A
Passionate
CALLING

Lloyd John
OGILVIE

HARVEST HOUSE PUBLISHERS
EUGENE, OREGON

Cover by Koechel Peterson & Associates, Inc., Minneapolis, Minnesota

A PASSIONATE CALLING
Copyright © 2014 by Lloyd John Ogilvie
Published by Harvest House Publishers
Eugene, Oregon 97402
www.harvesthousepublishers.com

Library of Congress Cataloging-in-Publication Data
    Ogilvie, Lloyd John.
    A passionate calling / Lloyd John Ogilvie.
       pages cm
    ISBN 978-0-7369-5487-7 (hardcover)
    ISBN 978-0-7369-5488-4 (eBook)
    1. Preaching. I. Title.
    BV4211.3.O35 2014
    251—dc23

2013023640

Printed in the United States of America

14 15 16 17 18 19 20 21 22 / LB-CD / 10 9 8 7 6 5 4 3 2 1

To Dr. Richard J. Mouw,
dynamic preacher, author, visionary theological educator,
prayer partner, and esteemed brother in Christ

Contents

Foreword

by Dr. Mark Labberton

Every Sunday was marked by two anticipations: that God would have a word and that the preacher would be ready to deliver it.

It was my first year at Fuller Theological Seminary. A good friend, Andy, and I drove the labyrinth of LA freeways each week from Pasadena to Hollywood to worship. By the weekend we were overfilled with seminary studies and were hungry to hear God's Word and to do so from a master preacher. The Rev. Dr. Lloyd John Ogilvie was then the pastor of First Presbyterian Church of Hollywood. Worship—we did. Preach—Lloyd did. Speak—God did. It was a weekly, life-giving feast.

Very few preachers have the rich baritone Lloyd does. But what's more, very few preachers give themselves to the task of preaching as Lloyd does. This arises for him not just as a commitment of the will, or a dedication to performance, but first and foremost as a passion of his heart.

When someone has the exceptional gifts of presence, and command, and sound that Lloyd Ogilvie has, it is possible to imagine that it would be easy to let those strengths just carry the day. In fact, some might rely on those gifts alone and neglect preparation, exegetical or spiritual. Lloyd did neither. Instead, what he gave week by week in his preaching was the harvest both of devotion and of hard work. "An hour in the study for every minute in the pulpit" was his watchword—and it was plain.

Lloyd's passion of the heart is the fire that burns in him. This is what enables his labor to be focused and purposeful, and the outcome of that labor to be in humble service of God's Word for the transformation of God's people. I remember the sheer pleasure and honor of listening to him preach, while also being struck as a pastor-in-training by the powerful combination of zeal and labor that lay behind how he did so. It was a rich, anticipated, weekly gift of grace.

All this contributed to my shock when, 33 years later, Fuller Theological Seminary asked me to consider becoming the Lloyd John Ogilvie Professor of Preaching and founding director of the Lloyd John Ogilvie Institute of Preaching. I am not Lloyd John Ogilvie! I couldn't imagine being in these positions when my own gifts seemed to me so different from his. In the surprising providence of God, however, the door opened, and I left serving as pastor of the beloved First Presbyterian Church of Berkeley to take these newly formed positions at Fuller.

In my early days at Fuller, Lloyd and I met to be together and to pray. The man I had only known from the balcony now became a brother in Christ. The enveloping voice and the penetrating eyes I had encountered from a distance became over time simply characteristics of this true friend. During the first two years I was at Fuller, I accompanied Lloyd as he led his Preaching with Passion conferences in Pasadena and beyond. Over and over again, I discovered that the combination of zeal and labor that had made such an impression years earlier continued to mark his life. The passion of and the passion for Jesus Christ motivated, filled, and empowered him—and, by grace, lives were changed.

Anyone who encounters Lloyd cannot help but be struck by his unique aura. Throughout his extraordinary service from Illinois, to Pennsylvania, to California, to Washington DC through his pastoral ministry; across the country through the weekly broadcast of *Let God Love You*; to the scores of his books, Lloyd has made an indelible mark. What he does, and how he does it, is impressive.

What has struck me time and again, however, is who Lloyd is—a genuine disciple, a lover of Christ, a student of Scripture, a servant of the church, a gentle and generous friend, a pastor of the mind and the heart. This explains what was evident to me from the balcony and now became known firsthand: the passion of Jesus Christ fills Lloyd Ogilvie, and this is the defining reality of Lloyd's life.

This book on the passion of preaching gives us marvelous windows into what Lloyd does in preaching and how he does it. Drink in these lessons, reflect on these practices, learn these habits. And, let the God who loves you make your life the sermon that you proclaim and preach. This will show you have inwardly digested what Lloyd John Ogilvie here teaches and exemplifies—that the passion of Jesus Christ you proclaim is your hope and the hope of the world.

Dr. Mark Labberton
President, Fuller Theological Seminary

Preface and Acknowledgments

G ratitude is a gift of grace. For me, it is the result of realizing that all that I am, have received, and have accomplished are evidences of the magnificent generosity of the goodness of God. I know that I could not breathe a breath, think a thought, write lucidly, compose a sermon, preach with passion, or write a book without the inspiration of God.

All that I want to communicate in this book about preaching with passion flows out of 64 years of a personal relationship with the Father through the passion of Christ and the power of the Holy Spirit.

One of the Lord's most gracious gifts is friendship with the people He puts in our lives, on time and in time, to help us accomplish what He has called us to do. What would we do without our friends? As I look back over my life, I am aware of how the Lord intervened through people He sent into my life to provide love, affirmation, wisdom, encouragement, courage, and accountability.

Throughout the pages of this book I want to introduce you to the loved ones, friends, professors, and fellow adventurers in living life to the fullest who have helped me claim the passionate calling of preaching the gospel.

When I retired as chaplain of the United States Senate in 2003, I had the pleasure of having lunch with my good friend Richard Mouw, then president of Fuller Theological Seminary. He expressed a hope that I would pass on what I had learned about preaching in my years of ministry. The offer of the possibility of establishing a chair of preaching and an institute of preaching in my name at Fuller was very moving.

Dr. Mouw explained the development of the Brehm Center for Worship, Theology and the Arts through the vision and generosity of William and Dee Brehm of Washington DC. He suggested that an Ogilvie Chair of Preaching and an Ogilvie Institute of Preaching should be part of the Brehm Center and that a distinguished preacher be selected to fill these two positions and be a part of the team of the Center and a member of the faculty of the seminary. Dr. Mouw also expressed the desire that the conferences on preaching I had planned to do throughout the nation as a concluding phase of my ministry be done through the Center.

This vision could not have been accomplished without the commitment, enthusiasm, and leadership of Sam Delcamp, then the executive director of The Fuller Foundation. Sam had been a faithful cheerleader during my years at the First Presbyterian Church of Hollywood, a member of the board of directors of Dunamis Christian Ministries, which guided my radio and television ministry, and a close, trusted friend. His provision of funds from the foundation to match money raised made it possible to establish the chair of preaching and the institute of preaching. I am grateful for all the friends throughout the nation who contributed to make the vision come true. The search for the Ogilvie Professor of Preaching was begun.

After an extensive search and countless interviews, a call was extended to Dr. Mark Labberton, then senior pastor of Berkeley Presbyterian Church. I had followed Mark's career, read his writings, and knew of his biblically rooted, Christ-centered, and Holy Spirit-inspired ministry. Most of all, I knew he was one of the truly great preachers in America. I was profoundly moved with gratitude that the Lord would send a person of Mark's talents and gifts to lead a movement to call, ignite, and equip a bold, brave, new breed of passionate preachers.

And talk about the gift of friendship! The Lord galvanized a great friendship between Mark and me right from our first time together as we shared our faith and our vision for the development of the calling to train potential preachers and renew the fire of passion in preachers in parishes throughout the nation. Since then Mark has become a wonderful prayer partner for my wife, Doris, and me.

I will always be grateful for the way Mark and I were able to work together on a series of Preaching with Passion conferences held nationwide. The messages I gave at these conferences became the basis of some of the chapters of this book.

Recently, Mark has been elected to be the new president of Fuller, following Richard Mouw. I can't think of a better choice. He combines the spiritual depth, intellectual acumen, relational skills, and administrative abilities to lead that benchmark seminary into the future.

And now my gratitude turns to you, my readers. I know many of you through the years of my travels to the small towns, villages, and metropolitan centers of the nation. You, together with new friends I hope to make as others of you read this book, are God's gracious gift to me.

I have tried to respond to many of you who have expressed the hope that when I wrote a book on preaching, I would include illustrations of portions, and even full copies, of sermons I have actually preached. As one man suggested, "Make it a 'show as well as tell' book!" That's exactly what I've tried to do.

Now, let's get on with our conversation about the most challenging and rewarding calling ever given to men and women: to preach with passion!

Lloyd John Ogilvie
March 2014

Chapter 1

The High Calling of a Preacher

This book is written as a conversation between the two of us. You and I share the very high calling to be preachers. Therefore, I believe we are numbered among the prophets, apostles, evangelists, and biblical scholar-preachers of the ages. Presumptuous? I don't think so.

An undeniable calling has put us there. Grace has kept us there. Supernatural power has been entrusted to us to make us impelling preachers there.

You and I have been conscripted to preach, and mandated with a message to preach with passion. We have been chosen to be communicators of the most stupendous good news ever entrusted to humankind.

Allow your mind to grasp it, free your emotions to soar with it, receive the full measure of God-esteem to take delight in it, make a fresh commitment to prioritize your life with an unreserved acceptance of it.

As a result of our preaching, people can come into personal relationship with God, the Creator, Sustainer, and Redeemer of the world. They can hear the healing, liberating news that they are loved and forgiven and can begin living an exhilarating life in Christ by accepting Him as their Lord and Savior. Their lives can be transformed and they can realize their full potential. They can be empowered by the Holy Spirit's wisdom, knowledge, and vision beyond what any amount of education or experience can provide.

Instead of just fleeting happiness, they can know lasting joy in life's excruciating suffering or difficulties. Superlative peace can be the source of their serenity in life's most triumphant or troublesome times.

They can discover how to pray and receive strength and courage to live life to the fullest. Their most urgent questions can be answered and their deepest needs can be met. They can experience healing of hurting memories, emotional pain, and physical disabilities.

And that's only the beginning. When we preach, people can receive their own personal call into the ministry of the laity. They can become communicators of grace to others and active workers for justice in the soul-sized issues of society. Marriages can be saved and families kept together. Profound bonds of friendship can be forged.

In the institutional church, faithful disciples can be set on fire, religious members who do not know God can be reached with the delight of living a dynamic, adventuresome faith, and dull worship services can be transformed into moving experiences of adoration, confession, and breathtaking hope.

Most humbling of all, through our preaching, people will come alive to live the abundant life now and live forever. Just imagine what it will be like when you and I graduate to heaven and meet the people who heard the gospel through us, accepted Christ as Lord and Savior, began adventuresome discipleship, and at the completion of this first phase of eternal life on earth, took the hand of the Savior and walked through the valley of the shadow of death and into the inexplicable glory of heaven!

This brief review of the impact of preaching makes me wonder where the wonder went in so many preachers' lives. How could preaching ever become mundane and boring? Or what's worse, how could preaching be moved so low on the list of what's really important in the parish ministry? For the congregation as well as the preacher!

Preaching has been devalued among the multiplicity of responsibilities of pastors. Little time is expected to be allotted to prayer and study in preparation of the sermon. Congregations often have become accustomed to preaching that is neither inspiring nor impelling. Expositional preaching of the Bible often is replaced by topical oratory that is little more than anecdotes threaded together on the thin thread of a popular theme to entertain or assure popularity.

Recovering Our Awesome Calling

What a great time for you and me to be countercultural leaders of a movement to recover the awesome calling of preaching! Our time yearns for scholar-preachers who are steeped in the Scriptures and committed to expository preaching, are sustained by the courage of bold biblical convictions, are strengthened by personal growth in prayer, and are sharpened by the dynamics and methods of intellectually stimulating, spiritually compelling, emotionally moving, and volitionally instigating communication.

> Our conversation in this book is a "trialogue." The Lord who called us to preach is with us— as I write these words and now as you are reading them.

It is not a trite oxymoron to say that the urgent need today is for preachers who really know Christ, are able to introduce people to Him, can help them grow in their knowledge of Him through weekly biblical sermons, and will sound His clarion call of them into the ministry of the laity.

Our time needs a bold, brave, new breed of clergy to lead the church as the twenty-ninth chapter of the book of Acts continues to be written! And why not? The urgent need is for you and me to accept the call to greatness in our preaching ministry.

And our response? Unless I miss my guess, you and I have several things in common. We long for a deeper relationship with Christ; we yearn for a fresh anointing of the Holy Spirit's supernatural gifts of wisdom, discernment, prophetic boldness, and courage; we want to press on in the pursuit of excellence in our preparation, presentation, and perfection of the skills of dynamic preaching; and we all have personal needs beneath the polished surface of our professionalism. Most of all, we need a reigniting of the fires of an authentic passion.

I really believe that our conversation in this book is a "trialogue." The Lord who called us to preach is with us—as I write these words and now as you are reading them. He will recall us to be heralds of His grace, He will melt the icy-cold fingers of fear that often grip our hearts, He will hammer any hardness in our wills that resists a character transplant into His likeness, He will mold our thinking around new goals for our preaching and fresh expectation of the miracles of changed lives He has planned to result from our preaching, He will vitalize our vision of what we can be and our congregations can become, and He will infuse us with contagious *charis* and *chara*, unqualified grace and unlimited joy!

And why? Because Christ loves the people to whom we preach—searching people who have never committed their lives to Him; religious people who need an intimate relationship with Him; church people who need to have their hearts set ablaze again; struggling people who need hope in tough times; and secular people who are searching for a faith that works in the secret anguishes of their hearts, in the struggles of marriage and the family, the shadowy ambiguities on the job in the asphalt jungle, and the soul-sized issues of our time.

This is our high calling!

Chapter 2

The Conscription of the Preacher

Allow me to be very personal in sharing my own conscription to preach. Really, it began when I was 15. That's not when I was called to preach, but when I first discovered the sheer delight of being a communicator. The calling to communicate grace came four years later.

My story begins at an ice-cream counter in a drugstore in Kenosha, Wisconsin. I was working as a "soda jerk," as we were called in those days. One evening I had my head down in the freezer sorting out the flavors of the pints of ice cream. Suddenly, I heard a strong, magnificently articulated voice say, "I want some ice cream!"

From inside the freezer I answered with my newly registered, deep but fluctuating post-puberty teenage voice, "What flavor, sir?"

"Never mind the flavor, who are you?" the voice demanded.

I pulled my head out of the ice-cream freezer and responded with a mixture of insecurity and lack of self-esteem, "I'm Lloyd Ogilvie."

"Where do you go to school?" the impressive, imposing man asked. I told him that I was a student at Mary D. Bradford High School, but that I was planning to quit and go to work in a factory.

"No, you're not going to quit, and I want to tell you why! In fact, I'll be back when you've finished work this evening and take you to my home, where you'll meet my wife, Verona, and she'll have some milk and cookies ready for us while we talk," the man said.

Sure enough, he was waiting for me when I finished work. At his home, while I was devouring the freshly baked cookies and cold milk his wife had prepared, he told me that he was John Davies, head of the speech department of my high school. I was both intrigued and awestruck when he told me that he wanted to train me to be in a speech contest the next month. He explained that he would teach me how to memorize a three-page speech for an oratorical declamation contest and would show me how to use my voice, how to stand, and how to gesture.

By the end of the visit and a plateful of cookies, I left with a sense of excitement about the future I had never experienced. The idea of quitting school was overcome with a desire to learn everything John Davies could teach me. Self-esteem and purpose began to surge within me.

Though I didn't realize it then, I had been recruited by one of the most outstanding speech teachers in the nation. He had trained many students who became famous speakers and actors in radio and the movies.

Every afternoon after regular classes, I met with Davies to go over the speech I was memorizing little by little. I stood at the center of an empty stage and repeated the speech over and over again, each time following new instructions he gave me as to how to move and gesture.

A month later, I traveled with fellow speech students to a contest in a nearby city. To this day I can remember how excited I felt when I gave my speech before an audience of students from the area—and most important of all, the judges who would decide who would be awarded first, second, third, and fourth places.

I was stunned when it was announced that I had won first place. "Congratulations!" my speech teacher said. And then, looking me in the eye, he said something I had never heard before: "I believe in you!"

That was the beginning. I felt the delight of being able to communicate as a speaker. Over the next four years, I continued my training, and in my senior year of high school was ready for original oratory. Now I had to decide what I wanted to say. The speech I drafted was delivered in contests throughout my state of Wisconsin and then in regional, and eventually national, competition. The American Legion Oratorical Contest provided me with a four-year scholarship to college.

All during this busy period of my life, I gave little thought to God. I was an agnostic when it came to any kind of faith. My plan was to go on in speech and dramatics with a career in radio (television was still undeveloped in 1948), and with a hope of a chance at acting and the movies. God, who overlooked my agnosticism, had other plans. He was on the move preparing the way in the choice of a college I thought was my independent decision. Not so.

The head of the speech department at Lake Forest College, Lake Forest, Illinois, came to see me as I was reviewing college choices and offered to have me use my scholarship there. It seemed like a good choice. Little did I know that it was God's choice.

When I arrived at Lake Forest College, I was assigned a dormitory room on the third floor of Durand Hall. The first person I met as I was struggling up the stairs pulling my trunk behind me was Bruce Larson, a senior student and the proctor of the dormitory. He helped me get settled and befriended me as I pressed on in my studies in speech and dramatics.

Bruce was also a speech major, so we had a lot in common. What I did not have in common with him was a faith in Jesus Christ. He had committed his life to Christ during the Battle of the Bulge as an army sergeant in World War II. He told me all about that as our friendship grew.

At that time, I also became good friends with Ralph Osborne, another senior who also had become a Christian during the war. Ralph had committed his life to Christ while serving on a battleship in the navy.

When Bruce and Ralph invited me to attend a Wednesday-evening Bible study and rap session in Bruce's room, I was intrigued and motivated to attend by the quality of their life-affirming, joyous, and contagious faith. In the weekly meetings, I heard about the exciting adventure of knowing and following Jesus Christ as Lord and Savior.

Six months later, after one of the sessions, Bruce and Ralph challenged me to turn over the control of my life to Christ and become His disciple. I returned to my room and, alone, struggled with that challenge. By four in the morning, on my knees, I finally choked out the words of a prayerful commitment to Christ as my Lord and Savior.

There were no flashing lights, bolts of lightning, or strains of beatific music, but a deep, gripping conviction that whatever else I did with my life, my passion was to be a disciple of Christ. Intellectually, I was convinced that Christ had died for me, forgiven me, and was calling me to serve Him first and foremost. Emotionally, I felt a surge of overwhelming love. Volitionally, I was liberated to surrender to Him my life and whatever talents had been entrusted to me. At this point, I assumed that meant being a Christian in the entertainment world. Once again, the Lord had other plans.

As I continued my studies in speech and dramatics, one day during my daily devotions I was profoundly moved by the desire for everyone to know the love, joy, and peace I had found in my growing relationship with Christ. I didn't hear an audible voice, but in the depth of my soul I heard the Lord say, *I want you to use the talents I have entrusted to you to speak to people about Me and what I have done in your life. Added to the talents I have given you on the human level, I will give you the supernatural gift of preaching. I am calling you into the ministry.*

Talk about a conscription and the motivation of a mandate! I could not have said "No!" even if I had wanted to. In point of fact, just the opposite was true. Everything within me shouted an enthusiastic "Yes!" I felt a Christ-induced fire of a passion to preach.

I accepted every chance I was offered to speak about Christ. The following year, I left my part-time job as a radio announcer and became a director of youth in a local church. Later, as I was completing college and seminary, I became a student pastor. The more I learned from the

Bible and studies in theology, the more excited I became about the privilege of preaching.

During my seminary years, I avidly read the writings of Dr. James Stewart and Dr. Thomas F. Torrance. Both were professors at New College, the University of Edinburgh, Scotland. The most fervent dream of my life was that someday I could study under these men. However, I did not have the financial resources to do that and dismissed the possibility. Once again, God had other plans.

One day Ruth Palmer, a teacher from my high school in Kenosha, Wisconsin, called me. She remembered my time as a student working with John Davies and had followed my progress through college and seminary. She asked me a very crucial question: "Is there something you feel led to do that you are not able to do? If so, I want to come and talk with you."

One afternoon, Ruth drove down from Kenosha to Gurnee, Illinois, where I was serving as a student pastor as I finished seminary. She brought with her a pen and a pad of paper on which she recorded my vision for the next step of my education. I told her about my hope of being able to study at New College. "What would it cost?" she asked.

I already had looked into that. I related the cost of transportation, food and housing, tuition, and books. As I detailed the expenses, I assumed she was simply making conversation expressing empathy and concern for a poor student. Instead she was writing down all of the detailed list of expenses. At the end of my recitation, she drew a line at the bottom of the list, added all the figures together, and came up with the total cost.

"Well," she exclaimed with delight, "That's about what I have saved to loan without interest to some student who would be willing to pay back the loan at one tenth a year for the first ten years after he completed his studies!" When I eagerly agreed to her generous terms, she wrote out a check for the amount that afternoon.

It was during my studies under Stewart and Torrance that I had an intellectual and spiritual opportunity to grow in my understanding of my calling to preach. At that point in my life, I needed to receive a much deeper experience of grace and the passion to preach with power.

I want to share with you a personal experience I had with Professor Stewart. He seemed to see into my soul with X-ray discernment. Even though I had been a Christian for several years when I arrived at New College, I lacked spiritual power. My fledgling years of schooling and student ministry had left me exhausted and in need of the very strength and courage I had tried to impart to others.

The passion I had experienced in the beginning of my faith journey was burning low. I needed a billowing of the embers in the hearth of my heart, a profound renewal. My theological orthodoxy had pinned me to the mat of self-generated piety. I was hammerlocked by the idea that my status with Christ was dependent on my performance. I had the words without the music; I was occupied with my studies about Christ, but needed the character transplant He had promised: "Abide in Me and I in you…apart from Me you can do nothing" (John 15:4-5 rsv).

Several deep conversations with Professor Stewart exposed my restless, self-justifying efforts to be good enough or work hard enough to earn Christ's love.

One day, Stewart met me in a corridor of New College. He looked me squarely in the eye, grasped my coat lapels, and talked intently about the essence of grace. He had read my examination "blue books" and knew I had the right words, but discerned I was not living the truth I wrote about. He concluded his explanation of grace with four liberating words: "You are loved *now!*"

I foolishly had put off living in the full measure of grace until I thought I deserved it. I discovered something I have had to relearn again and again through the years: an ever-deepening experience of grace opens the floodgate for ever-increasing passion in preaching.

This personal encounter with Professor Stewart prepared me for a very moving experience a few days later in his class. His lecture that day was on John chapter 14. He spoke about the present, indwelling power of Christ as our living contemporary. Our lives, he said forcefully, were to be Christ's postresurrection home. With a fine blend of exegesis, exposition, and scholarship, plus classical and contemporary illustrations of people who had experienced the power of the indwelling Christ, Dr. Stewart vividly described what it meant to abide in Christ and for Christ to abide in us. The truth reignited a fire within me that had been banked.

> "If we could but show the world that being committed to Christ is...the most exciting adventure the human spirit can know—those who have been standing outside the church and looking askance at Christ will come crowding in..."

Before Professor Stewart ended his lecture, he paused, whipped off his glasses, and stood looking out the window as if transfigured by Christ Himself. Then, in crisp, staccato words so characteristic of his passionate preaching and teaching, he said something that transformed my vision of preaching for the rest of my life: "If we could but show the world that being committed to Christ is no tame, humdrum, sheltered monotony—but the most exciting adventure the human spirit can know—those who have been standing outside the church and looking askance at Christ will come crowding in to receive His grace, experience forgiveness, become new creatures, and be filled with His indwelling Spirit. And we may well expect the greatest revival since Pentecost!"

Stewart concluded with his firm conviction of Christ's indwelling, transforming power in us. And then he asked a question: "And why not?" After a pause, he looked at each of us in the eye and pressed for a verdict, "And why not *you?*"

The question throbbed in my heart. I was stirred profoundly and decided then and there that I wanted to be part of that revival. I committed my life to live in the flow of Christ's supernatural power and preach with passion.

Now all I needed was an expression from the laity about the longing for passionate preaching in the church. You guessed it: the Lord already had plans for that.

A short time after I returned from my studies in Scotland, a committee of men from Winnetka, Illinois, came to see me. They represented a group of people in their suburb of Chicago who were organizing a new Presbyterian church. The spokesman of the delegation made me an offer: "If you will tell us about Christ, we'll help you organize your life!" These leaders of the Chicago business world offered to teach me what they knew about goal-oriented management. As a 26-year-old, I really needed what they offered, and I could see that they were in earnest about their desire to know Christ.

That desire was fervently expressed as I began my ministry as their pastor. The church began with 130 members and grew rapidly as others who longed to know Christ personally joined the adventure of being His disciples.

One Christmas Eve, I received a memorable expression of the congregation's persistent desire for me to preach Christ. The construction of a sanctuary was completed and ready for the first worship service in it. The building committee made a mysterious request that I not see the new pulpit in the chancel until just before I preached the first sermon in the new sanctuary.

I'll never forget the mixture of emotions I felt as I followed the choir down the center aisle during the hymn of adoration. I was astonished to see that a large tarpaulin covered the pulpit. It remained over the pulpit all through the adoration, confession, supplication, and intercession portions of the celebration worship. Then it was time to read the Scripture and preach.

My heart thumped faster as the tarpaulin was raised. What I saw was a magnificently carved pulpit with a large lectern at the center with a pulpit Bible on it. My excitement grew as I stepped into the pulpit.

Then a chill went up my spine as I looked down at the Bible and the lectern. Carved into the lectern just below where the Bible rested were the words spoken to Philip by the Greeks who were seeking an audience with Jesus: *"Sir, we wish to see Jesus."*

I was so moved by this reminder by the members of the church of the deepest longing of their hearts and the most urgent quest of their minds, that I stood silent for what must have seemed like an hour to the congregation. A lump formed in my throat and tears streamed down my face. In those divinely inspired moments, I remembered what I have shared with you in this chapter: my first experience of Christ, my quest to know Him more intimately, my call to preach with passion, and my commitment to study and preparation to communicate abundant and eternal life…and that preaching the Word could change the lives of people.

Then, in the echo chamber of my mind came the reverberation of two quotations I had memorized and sought to make my motto. One was by Nicholas von Zinzendorf: "I have one passion only: it is He! It is He!" The other was by Charles H. Spurgeon: "We have a great need for Christ and a great Christ for our needs!"

Now, many years after that memorable Christmas Eve, I seldom enter a pulpit to preach without remembering the clarion call of those words, "Sir, we wish to see Jesus!"

For me, the primary goal of preaching is to proclaim the exciting adventure of knowing Christ. It is to communicate the astounding message of His prevenient desire to have us know Him, His persistent search for us, His profound love for us, His propitious forgiveness offered to us, His power to transform our lives, His presence with us to give us strength and courage, His plan for us to live an unfettered life that difficulties cannot diminish or death destroy, and His provision for us to live forever in heaven with Him.

Breathtaking, isn't it? That's why we were born and reborn: to respond to both Christ's call and the longing of people for passionate preaching. Who is up to responding? Are you? Am I? No, not on our own strength, of course. But be aware—the Lord is raiding the ranks of preachers in all denominations. You and I are meant to be among those He conscripts and mandates to preach with passion!

Chapter 3

The Passion of the Preacher

Dwight L. Moody was right. "The best way to revive a church is to build a fire in the pulpit." And I say that fire must begin in the heart of the man or woman who stands in that pulpit. You and I need that fire to be preachers with passion.

Let's be clear about what we mean by passion. We face an etymological challenge because of the misuse of the word in our day. We need to reject one contemporary definition of passion, the definition that is limited to sex. Fortunately, the dictionary broadens our scope: "strong feelings of love, anger, or desire." We are still on the surface.

We must press deeper to discover the meaning of *passion* in the Greek New Testament. *Paschō*, the Greek verb, is directly related to Christ's suffering on the cross. Acts 1:3 is a fulcrum text: "He [Christ] presented Himself alive after His suffering [*pathein*] by many infallible proofs." Here *pathein* is the second aorist active of *paschō*. *Pathein* is also used in Acts 17:3 and 26:23 for Christ's suffering, His substitutionary, vicarious sacrifice for the sins of the world.

But press on! *Passion* in the Greek New Testament also is used for the suffering of the first-century followers of Christ. Paul uses a compound word, *sunpaschōmen*, to "suffer with Christ." In Romans 8:17 suffering with Christ is the secret of being glorified with Him (*sundoxasthōmen*). "The Spirit Himself bears witness with our spirit that we are children of God, and if children, then heirs—heirs of God and joint heirs with Christ, if indeed we suffer with Him, that we may also be glorified together." The "if" better could be translated "since." There is nothing conditional about suffering with Christ or being glorified with Him when we do.

Allow me to suggest a definition of passion. It is profound love produced in us by God's love for us, inspiring a fresh experience of His grace, accepting Christ's suffering for us and receiving forgiveness. This liberating realization produces an in-depth empathy in us for the suffering of others. Three realities are inseparable in authentic passion: *Ta pāthé toú Christu*, Christ's suffering; *Ta pathé ma*, my suffering; *Ta pathé ma tatous*, their suffering.

Authentic passion is understood and experienced in what my theological mentor, the late Dr. Thomas Torrance, called the "glory circle of the Trinity." The Father glorifies the Son and the Son glorifies the Father and the Holy Spirit, and then the Holy Spirit draws us into the circle to share with Him and the Son in the glorification of the Father.

In his benchmark book *The Mediation of Christ*, I found in printed form some of the stunning truths I had heard Dr. Torrance teach in a classroom of New College:

> It is through the incarnation and atonement effected by the conjoint activity of Christ and the Holy Spirit that God has opened the door for us to enter into His holy presence and know Him as He really is in His triune being. In this two way movement of atoning propitiation whereby God draws near to us and draws us near to Himself, the access to the Father given to us through the grace of the Lord Jesus Christ and in the communion of the Holy Spirit is such that we are enabled, quite astonishingly and beyond any worth or capacity of our own, to participate, creaturely beings though we are, in eternal communion and inner relations of knowing and loving within God Himself.[1]

Passionate Preaching

Passionate preaching is engendered in intimacy in the glory circle. Let the word *intimacy* stand. It really means the union that takes place when the real *I* meets and communes with the true God in the interaction of the Persons of the Trinity. We are given the gift of living in the essence of the Father's love, revealed when He did not spare His own Son, who was part of His innermost Heart and self-giving nature, but gave Him up for us all in the atoning sacrifice of the cross. He loved humankind more than Himself!

In the glory circle, Christ takes us by the hand and presents us to the Father: "Here, Father, this chosen and called preacher has received the Holy Spirit's gift of faith to believe in the atonement You provided in the cross. Now he (she) needs to experience our constant, timeless, exchange of love, and to accept that You love him (her) *as much as You love Me.* Help him (her) to receive that sublime love, and know how much We loved him (her) when I hung on the cross centuries before he (she) was born, so that he (she) can be a communicator of that same love, and can become all that We had in mind for him (her) when we first thought of him (her) before the beginning of time."

Astonishing? Yes! A passion born and nurtured in the glory circle is so much more profound than an aloof intellectual reflection on the atonement. Read Jesus' prayer for us recorded in John 17 and relish our oneness (intimacy) with Him as He eternally talks to the Father about you and me.

Our part of this intimacy is to be totally honest and open with Christ without pretense or assumed piety. Daily. On some days, hourly. He will not draw into the glory circle a fictitious person of our own making and faking. Phony clerical presumption must be discarded for integrity and intentionality. We can keep short accounts with Christ in the flow of His fresh grace.

Grace-motivated passion for preaching is received daily, and then during our preaching, as we confess our needs, failures, frustrations, and inadequacies and experience the love we cannot earn or deserve. Filled with wonder and praise, we will speak the truth in a winsome, winning expression of the love we witnessed and received, and are receiving moment by moment in the ecstasy of the glory circle. Once again, let the word *ecstasy* stand. It means intense joy and delight. That's exactly what Christ promised.

Every time I enter a pulpit to preach, in my mind's eye I imagine my hand reaching out to grasp the nail-pierced hand of Christ, receiving His healing love for my deepest hurts and hopes, and then with the other hand reaching out to the people to whom I will preach, remembering that I am one with them in their struggles and their anxieties, but also as recipient of the freedom and joy the Lord is ready to give us together in the sacred time of the sermon. Allow me to explain further.

Passionate preaching is allowing our minds and hearts to become crucibles for compounding our own experience of Christ's unqualified, unmerited, unfettered love with our identification and involvement with the sometimes expressed, but often hidden, suffering of people. Poet Pietro Metastasio was right: "If every man's internal care were written on his brow, how many would our pity share who raise our envy now?"

But don't miss the astounding promise that when we suffer with Christ we'll also be glorified with Him. As we share in His passionate love for people who desperately need Him, we will be glorified with Him. Here glorification is so much more than being complimented or extolled. The glory of the Lord is the revelation and manifestation of His presence and all that He is ready to provide.

You and I are meant to be glorified preachers! Don't resist the wonder of that in some kind of false facsimile of humility. The promise is clear: if we suffer with Christ we will be glorified with Him. For me, that means death to self-centered aggrandizement and an unreserved commitment to be to the people to whom we preach what Christ has been to us. It means resurrection to a new, Christ-captivated, gifted person with knowledge beyond our intellectual abilities, inspirational insight into the Scriptures beyond our expositional training, X-ray discernment of people's needs beyond our presuppositions, radiance beyond personality prowess, illustrative stills beyond the reach of our research, stunning writing, memorization, and speaking strengths beyond our training, and yes, divinely inspired humor beyond trite jokes. All results of the supernatural manifestation of the presence of the Lord in a human being called to preach with passion!

A glorified preacher is a living miracle of the Trinity: the Father's approbation of grace through His Son and the Spirit's appropriation of power to maximize our human talent and training with the magnitude of supernatural gifts. There must be a *chrism* (anointing) that results in authentic *charisma* (grace-giftedness). Check the alpha in the Greek. For the passionate, glorified preacher there must be a chrism before charisma!

Nothing can happen through us until it happens to us. We can communicate only what is real to us through fresh experiences of grace.

The Focus of True Passion

Christ Himself is the focus of true passion. The context of the gospel is the source of the stirring convictions that stimulate our passion. We must be centered on the *kerygma* and the *didache*, the proclamation and the teaching, of the New Testament. We need to live in the ethos of the first-century church and its essential message focused on the preexistent Christ, the divine Word of God, the incarnate Son, the suffering, crucified Savior, the risen Victor over Satan and death, the triumphant, reigning Lord, and the baptizer with the Holy Spirit. Oscar Cullmann said, "It is the *present* Lordship of Christ, inaugurated by His resurrection and exaltation to the right hand of God, that is the center of the faith of primitive Christianity."

It is also the center of a passionate preacher's study. We come from our time of study and prayer with the undeniable conviction that what happened to the followers and disciples of Jesus and the early Christians can mysteriously but undeniably be recapitulated in the lives of people today.

We preach with passion when we have listened to the deepest needs and most urgent questions of people, when we have their anxieties and worries on our hearts, when we enter into their problems and perplexities, their agonies and anguishes, and when we realize that without Christ they cannot live life to the fullest now and in heaven for eternity.

But there is something more that is the source of preaching with passion. It is the biblical assurance that Christ changes people. The conviction that fires our preaching is that when we come to be in Christ, the old passes away and the new comes. People can be changed! *Metanoia* and *metamorphoō,* repentance and transformation, are inseparably related. Repentance, to change our minds from self-reliance and self-justification, makes possible a transformation of a person's character, personality, attitudes, values, goals, and objectives. An old self in bondage to pride, self-centeredness, and fear can be transformed!

The faces of people who have been changed by Christ over the 60 years of my experience of preaching stream before my mind's eye. Young and old, rich and poor, successful and struggling—all people who needed to be transformed by Christ, and through the miracle of preaching were able to confess their need, receive the gift of faith, commit their lives to Christ, be filled with the Holy Spirit, and begin the exciting adventure of discipleship.

> "Never forget…you are working for a verdict. You are hoping and praying to leave your people face-to-face with God in Christ."

James Denny used to say that our theologians should be evangelists and our evangelists theologians. We need preachers who are both.

Richard Baxter's words always were on the door by which I entered the chancel of churches I've served: "I preach as a dying man to dying men and women as if never to preach again." A great reminder of my purpose. Baxter's appeal to preachers was, "I earnestly beseech you all in the name of God and for the sake of your people's souls, that you will not slightly slubber over this work, but do it vigorously and with all your might and make it your great and serious business." We must be so immersed in the Scriptures that our preaching comes out of us flaming and burning with urgency.

James Stewart, my professor of New Testament Theology at New College, University of Edinburgh about whom I spoke in the previous chapter, gave me a mandate for the ministry of preaching: "The preacher of the gospel is essentially a herald of the most magnificent and moving tidings that ever broke upon the world, the mighty acts of God in and through His Word, the Mediator. What was the essence of the proclamation of the original heralds of the faith? They proclaimed that prophecy was fulfilled, that in Jesus of Nazareth, in His words and deeds, His life and resurrection, the kingdom of God had arrived, that God had exalted Him, that He would come again as Judge, and that now was the day of salvation.

"Never forget," Stewart went on, "You are working for a verdict. You are hoping and praying to leave your people face-to-face with God in Christ." That goal must never be preempted. Preaching is not the propagation of gentle views, but the proclamation of good news. The purpose of our scholarship is not the gathering of esoteric ideas to be discussed with erudite language, but to prepare for the sermon as a divinely intended encounter where women and men become acutely aware of the Lord's presence and where a worshipping congregation will forget about the preacher and be confronted and comforted by the living Christ."

Then people will be able to say of the passionate preacher,

> 'Twas not just the words you spoke
> To you so clear, to me so dim,

> But 'twas that when you preached
> You brought a sense of Him.
> In your eyes He beckoned me
> And in your smile His love was spread
> Until I lost sight of you
> And saw the Lord instead!

Preaching Christ, the Word of God, *is* the Word of God. Our calling is to respond to Paul's admonition to Timothy, "Preach the Word!" (2 Timothy 4:2). He not only was called to preach, but to preach the Word. An old Latin phrase is our motto: *"Predicatio verbi divini est verbum divinum,"* the preaching of the Word of God is the Word of God! This conviction gives verve and vitality to scholarship and consequently to preaching. Do we really believe that in preaching the Scriptures expositionally, the living God confronts people in judgment and mercy and offers to them through Christ the gift of eternal life? We not only speak *about* God, but in a very real sense, *for* God.

Our Calling

The need of the hour is to confirm John Calvin's conviction:

> The Word goeth out of the mouth of God in such a manner
> that it likewise goeth out of the mouth of men; for God does
> not speak openly from heaven but employs men as His instruments…It is a singular privilege that He designs to consecrate
> to Himself the mouths and tongues of men [I would add, "and
> women"] in order that His voice may resound in them.

The realization that an exposition of a verse or portion of the Bible, empowered by the Holy Spirit, will be the Word of God to the congregation energizes and encourages us as preachers. It also relieves us of the dreadful assumption that we are dependent on human resources alone to cajole and convince reluctant listeners. My prayer is that you and I will never lose our wonder over this mystery and our awe that the Word of God will be spoken through us. This will fire the passion so urgently needed in our preaching.

We have been called to an exciting adventure. We must experience what we exposit. Once more for emphasis: we never can bypass the undeniable axiom—*Nothing can happen through us that has not happened to us, and we can communicate to others only what we have freshly rediscovered in our own thought and experience.*

I agree with Bishop William A. Quayle, an American Methodist bishop of a previous generation:

> Preaching is the art of making a sermon and delivering it. Why no, that is not preaching. Preaching is the outpouring of the soul in speech. Therefore, the elemental business in preaching is not with preaching but with the preacher. It is no trouble to preach, but a vast trouble to construct a preacher. What then, in the light of this, is the task of a preacher? Mainly this, the amassing of a great soul so as to have something worthwhile to give— the sermon is the preacher up to date.

Our calling is to allow the biblical text or passage to have its full impact on us. As passionate preachers we have the privilege of living in the passage and let it speak to us before we speak about it to the congregation. We can lead others only so far as we have gone ourselves; we cannot give away what we don't have. Truth and reality, faith and experience, discovery and application, never should be separated.

Four crucial convictions are the quadraphonic drumbeats of great preaching and the sources of our true passion—unconditional grace through the cross, union with Christ, the character transplant that takes place when a person becomes His postresurrection home, and the thrilling call to be His disciples.

The unqualified, unfettered, unlimited love of God in Christ must thunder forth with the passion of one who knows the reality of being preveniently loved and forgiven. Rembrandt painted his own face in the crowd at the foot of the cross in his painting of the crucifixion. We must write and then preach the reality of the cosmic atonement of Calvary as men and women saved by grace alone.

A cartoon pictured a clergyman being carried out of the front door of a church on the shoulders of his parishioners. One observer asked, "I wonder what that's all about?" "Oh, nothing," another responded. "He just preached a sermon saying that sin does not matter." And yet it does matter, and people long for a word from the Lord about their feeling of alienation from Him and His grace. They are not free.

Our calling is to make the vital reality of forgiveness so undeniably clear that no one will miss it. The apostle Paul gives us an illuminating illustration of forgiveness in his letter to the Colossians. He pictures the Colossians' sins as a charge list.

In ancient times charges were listed out against a person, and if he signed it, that was an admission in his own hand of his debt. The Greek word for a charge list was *cheirographon,* meaning an autograph, a note of hand, a bond signed by a debtor acknowledging his indebtedness. In Paul's time, people wrote on papyrus, made of the pith of bulrushes, or on vellum, made of the skin of animals. The ink used then had no acid in it and therefore did not penetrate indelibly into the fiber of the paper. A sponge could wipe it away as if it had never existed on the surface. When debts were paid or charges exonerated, a nail cutting through the list was a seal for all to observe of the cancellation of the debt or charge.

In that context, we can picture what a radical redemption Paul wanted to portray: "You, being dead in your trespasses...He [God] has made alive together with Him [Christ], having forgiven you all trespasses, having wiped out the handwriting of requirements that was against us, which was contrary to us. And He has taken it out of the way, having nailed it to the cross" (Colossians 2:13-14). The Greek word for canceled is *exaleipho,* from the verb *exaleiphein,* "to wipe off, wipe away, obliterate, erase."

The vivid picture is of God taking the grace sponge of atonement and wiping out all the charges and incriminating memory of failure. The picture further flashes our liberation as it depicts God wrenching the charge list out of our clutched hands and nailing it to the cross. He has taken it completely away from us. It is not ours anymore.

When the nails were driven through Christ's hands and feet, all our sins were crucified with Him. Our sins and failures were cut clean through by the nails that caused the Savior such anguish. Christ took the sins of the world, then and now, when He cried, "It is finished!" He declared not only the finished work of redemption, but also the finish of our self-condemnation. What else should be finished is our reluctance and often refusal at times to forgive others.

As we look out on our congregations we know that every Sunday there are people there who need the charge list wrenched from their hands. There are others who need to forgive themselves. And be sure of this: most everyone needs to forgive someone. It is sheer arrogance to refuse to forgive another person for what the Lord has already forgiven. Our people will not be free until they are willing to accept their own forgiveness, forgive themselves, and forgive others.

There is a great need for preaching forgiveness because most people, preachers included, have a better memory of past failures than God has chosen to have. We tend to be far less gracious to ourselves and others than He is. That's blasphemy! We harbor the mistakes and misdeeds long after we have heard and seemingly accepted the good news of the gospel. We continue to assume the responsibility for our justification even though God has assumed it once and for all on Calvary.

> Down beneath the shame and loss
> Sinks the plummet of the cross:
> Never yet abyss was found
> Deeper than His love could sound.
> I sometimes think about the cross,

And close my eyes to see
The cruel nails and crown of thorns
And Jesus crucified for me.
But even could I see Him die
I could but see a little part
Of that great love, which, like a fire,
Is always burning in His heart.[2]

Passion indeed!

As preachers, we must be tenaciously gripped by this message and allow it to become the driving motivation of our preaching. All our human talents, education, and experience, multiplied by the gift of preaching from the Holy Spirit, must be focused to help our congregations understand the gift of forgiveness.

There is great power in our proclamation of prevenient grace. People will hear not just our voices, but the whisper of the Spirit in their souls, reminding them that God's grace is always beforehand with them, love that is given before it is either deserved or even asked for.

Our goal as passionate preachers is to call and inspire the laity to run with the Master on a two-legged gospel. The indicative of the gospel carries a life-changing imperative. All circumstances of life are to be impacted by the changed women and men who receive, by our preaching, the high calling of the ministry of the laity. To be in Christ is to be in ministry. We do not need to send people into the structures of society; they already are there! Our preaching is to enlist, enable, and equip them to live out their faith in their relationships and responsibilities.

That requires passion in the pulpit. That ever-deepening passion grows in the preacher through prolonged and penetrating prayer. Next we turn our attention to prayer as our source of our sufficiency for any effectiveness in preaching.

Chapter 4

The Prayer Life of the Preacher

"Do you love to preach?" Dr. Harrison Ray Anderson, then pastor of Fourth Presbyterian Church in Chicago, asked me before the Presbytery of Chicago as part of an examination for ordination.

"Oh, yes, sir!" I responded with enthusiasm. Dr. Anderson smiled and then asked, "Do you love the people to whom you preach?"

I answered this second question with the same enthusiasm as the first. However, the penetrating implications of this second question have remained with me all through the years.

Preaching is an act of love. The hours of preparation, writing, and memorization, and the actual time in the pulpit are all responses of love for God in the glory circle. Out of the overflow of that love, a profound love for our congregation becomes an undeniable, outward expression. People will listen to a preacher they know loves them. This love is expressed in the many aspects of pastoral care, of course, but sublimely in passionate preaching in the pulpit. The expression of our faces, the look in our eyes, the tone of our voices, and the total impression of our body language may affirm or contradict what we are trying to communicate.

A friend of mine attended a worship service with his young son. As they walked out of the sanctuary, the little boy tugged his dad's hand and exclaimed, "Why was that preacher so mad at us?" The preacher had been preaching on grace! The lad felt his anger and not grace.

We've all had times when what we really were thinking or feeling spoke so loudly that our people did not hear what we were preaching.

There is no profession that requires more inner spiritual and psychological health than preaching. All of the methods of mental health and spiritual healing must be practiced each day of the week before we enter the pulpit on Sunday. Any unresolved hurts, angers, broken relationships, or guilt must be resolved or they will ooze into our outward persona while we are preaching the good news of the gospel.

When I was pastor of the First Presbyterian Church of Hollywood, I had a group of church elders who would meet with me every Sunday morning for prayer. Before they would gather around me for the laying on of hands for a renewed anointing for the awesome privilege of preaching, one of the elders would ask, "For what may we pray? What is your greatest hope for the sermon today? What do you need from the Lord now before you preach? Is there anything between you and the Lord or with any other person or situation that would keep you from being maximum for the Lord in preaching today?" Often I would share the thrust of the message and then any worries or concerns that would distract me from being focused in proclaiming the Word of the Lord. Those prayer times were invaluable.

But these prayers did not substitute for my daily prayers for my congregation. Generalized prayer is the enemy of personalized and particularized prayer. The church officers (whatever they are called in your denomination) should be prayed for every day, followed by specific prayers for people in need, and then a segment of the list of members. Dividing the membership roll into a group for each day's time of intercessory prayer will produce a greater empathy before we begin our studies and sermon preparation.

> The power of this time of prayer produces the intimacy with Christ we've talked about...and makes us radiant with His passion and glory.

It is the power of this time of prayer that produces the intimacy with Christ we've talked about in previous chapters and makes us radiant with His passion and glory for our preaching. We will be able to preach with great power what has become real to us in our prayers. Through prayer, Christ infuses all the faculties of our cerebral cortex, providing supernatural vision and discernment; His Spirit flows through our limbic systems, enabling strength and endurance; His power engenders energy through our sympathetic adaptation systems; His character is transplanted into our personality. For us, Christianity is life as Christ lived it, life as we live it in Him, and life as He lives it in us (read John 15 at least once a week!).

How and What to Pray

You may be wondering about how and what to pray for your people. Rather than just going down a list, I found it helpful to be sure of what I wanted to ask the Lord for their lives, and ask Him how I could be sure I was on His agenda and keeping straight His priorities.

I found it helpful consistently to reread 2 Corinthians chapter three. Paul loved his friends in Corinth and not only admonished them, but affirmed them. I found that rereading this chapter reoriented my thinking about my ministry, and particularly my preaching. It helped me refocus the goal, grace, gallantry, and glory of passionate preaching.

The apostle Paul clearly asserts that changed lives are the goal of ministry. He tells the Corinthians that they are his epistles, known and read by others. In the context of our emphasis that the primary function of our ministry is the preaching of the gospel, we claim the assurance that Christ changes people. As we noted in the previous chapter, this conviction fires our preaching with passion. When people come to be in Christ, the old passes away and the new comes. So our prayer for our preaching begins with intercession for the beloved men and women to whom we preach.

We preach with the indicative to proclaim the gospel, but also with the present passive imperative used so forcefully by Paul. Note Romans 12:2: "Do not be conformed to this world, but be transformed"—both *sunschematizesthe* and *metamorphousthe* are in the present passive imperative—the liberation from conformity and the transformation is for now and is done to us; and yet it should be earnestly sought. The same is true for Ephesians 5:18, also in the present passive imperative—"Keep on being filled with the Spirit" (author's translation).

Those in our congregations to whom we preach represent a spectrum of people. Some need conversion, others need to take the next step in their growth, others are facing immense problems and are in need of encouragement, others are suffering physically or emotionally, others are lonely, and still others are confronting complex decisions and need hope to press on.

As we preach, like Paul, we will be writing our epistles in our people and all those around them will read them. The goal of our preaching is to send epistles of Christ's transforming power into the world. Can we say to our people as Paul did to the Corinthians, "You are manifestly an epistle of Christ, ministered by us, written not on tablets of stone, but on tablets of flesh, that is, of the heart"?

Our Transformation Through Prayer

For that goal we need grace. Who can meet all the varied needs of the multiplicity of people who listen to our preaching? Who is sufficient for that? Paul's answer was tried and tested in the crucible of challenging ministry:

> Not that we are sufficient of ourselves to think of anything as being from ourselves, but our sufficiency is from God, who has made us sufficient as ministers of the new covenant, not of the letter but of the Spirit; for the letter kills, but the Spirit gives life (2 Corinthians 3:5-6).

The Greek word Paul uses, which is translated as *sufficient* in our English versions, is *hikanotes*, from the verb *hikanoo*, meaning "competent or to be made able." It is interesting to note that the Jewish interpretation of the name of God, El Shaddai, the Almighty, was sometimes explained to mean "The Sufficient One."

Paul asserts that the all-sufficient One has made him sufficient for his ministry. He points away from himself to the Lord who has made it possible for those who were impacted by his ministry to be his epistles of testimony to their changed lives.

The same can be true for us. In daily prayer in preparation for preaching and then in moment-by-moment prayer as we preach, the Lord will make us sufficient. The triumphant shout of Paul was not "I am able," but "He is able!" Prayer enables this confidence, this *tharsos*, Christ promised (John 16:33—*tharseite*: "have courage"), and imputes as a special gift for otherwise inadequate preachers like you and me.

Because of the confidence of this sufficiency, Paul could claim a glorious ministry greater than Moses. Unashamedly, so can we! Consider the fading glory on the face of Moses, and then consider the assurance we have: "Since we have such hope, we use great boldness of speech—unlike Moses, who put a veil over his face so that the children of Israel could not look steadily at the end of what was passing away" (2 Corinthians 3:12-13).

For us preachers, this means that prayer results in an unfading glory—manifestation—of the Spirit in us. Our intimacy with the Lord produces what Paul claimed—great boldness of speech. Here boldness is *parresia* in the Greek text: *par* from *pas*—all or highest degree or the maximum; and *rehesis* from "speech," meaning freedom of speech, unreservedness of utterance, to speak without ambiguity or fear, but with confidence and courage. Boldness marked the movement of the early church. It is also the sure sign that as preachers we have spent time in prayer each day. This is the source of the radiance of the glory of the Lord.

One Sunday morning when I was the pastor in Hollywood, a woman greeted me after one of the worship services. What she intended to say came out all wrong: "Every sermon you preach is better than the next!" When she realized what she had said, happily she laughed and reworded it into the affirmation she intended.

Later that Sunday afternoon, I reflected on the woman's befuddled comment. What she actually said touched a deep concern I have had all through my ministry. The longing of my heart is to press on in ever-increasing experience of the glory of the Lord through prolonged daily prayer and have that glory radiant in my preaching. Through the Lord's sufficiency, I want every sermon to be better than the *last*!

One of the greatest discoveries I made early in my ministry was that I needed daily reading and study of the Scriptures for my own relationship with the Lord before I would prayerfully launch into the in-depth prayer and study of the text on which I was planning to preach the following Sunday. The temptation many preachers face is to use the sermon preparation time as a substitute for their own devotional reflection on a portion of Scripture and prayer to ask the Lord to apply it to their own lives. The Lord must get through to us in personal prayer before we prepare sermons to seek to get through to our congregations in our preaching.

Don't miss the emphasis of this in Paul's thought here in 2 Corinthians chapter three. In prayer, we are given freedom of access to the Lord. "The Lord is the Spirit; and where the Spirit of the Lord is, there is liberty. But we all, with unveiled face, beholding as in a mirror the glory of the Lord, are being transformed into the same image from glory to glory, just as by the Spirit of the Lord" (2 Corinthians 3:18).

R.C.H. Lenski comments,

> On the face of Moses the glory of the judgment of God was reflected; on our face the Lord's gospel is to be reflected. Already this much, namely becoming a mirror, which reflects the brilliant sunrays of Christ's glory of grace and salvation. But in all of us who have turned to the Lord there is vastly more. A mirror

only reflects. Moses' face only reflected. His face, like a mirror, remained only what it was. Christ's glory of grace enters into us, transforms, metamorphoses, us "into the same image from glory to glory." The verb is passive: "we are being transformed," namely by the Lord's Spirit; it is present and durative: the transformation begins with the new birth (John 3:3,5), and continues in sanctification through life (John 17:17). It has been well said that this transformation is *spiritualis* and not *essentialis.* We remain we, the Lord remains the Lord. Hence Paul writes, "into the same image," the image of the glory of the Lord which we reflect.[3]

Now consider the implication of all this for our preaching. With this quality of prayer, we come face to Face, that is, person to Person with the Lord, and we are being changed into His likeness. With a glory radiant on our faces, expressed in our attitudes, exuded by our body language and, most of all, exposed in the gifts of insight, discernment, and wisdom, we do not need to fear Moses' problem of fading glory. We will be able to preach with courage.

"Courage," said Karle Wilson Baker, "is fear that has said its prayers." It is the special gift for an impelling proclamation of the gospel. Courage is something we take because the Lord has taken hold of us. Courage is the power to overcome rather than being overcome. Christ's assurance should be printed out and put above our computer screens: "Take courage! I have overcome the world" (John 15:33, author's translation).

I have a Scots friend who ends most every conversation by saying, "Tak courage, lad—it's yours, ya know!"

That's only partly true. Christ is the source of true courage. With His courage, we will be preachers with unveiled faces in the pulpit communicating the gospel without fear! Think of it: no longer a fear of failing our Lord, no more edgy anxiety about losing power in the pulpit, no more worry over missing the mark of our high calling; and no more compulsive efforts to meet the varied expectations of our people. We do not need to be paranoid puppets or people-pleasers. What a delight! We are free of demands to be more conservative or liberal politically, more fundamentalist or evangelical, and more radical or revolutionary. The popularity contest, with jolly smiles until our teeth get dry, is over. We can be the new, real, transformed persons the Lord is creating and empowering. No need for a veil of presumed piety or spiritual superiority to hide a fading glory! What a relief!

Intimate Prayer

The quality of intimate prayer that results in the ever-increasing glory of the Lord in our lives is dialogical: it begins with the Lord. He is the initiator. "It shall come to pass that before they call, I will answer; and while they are still speaking, I will hear" (Isaiah 65:24). We respond with praise, the thermostat of our spirit that opens us up to receive what the Lord has prepared in the ups and downs of our lives. Praise is the liberating level of relinquishment and release. When we begin praising the Lord for who He is and all that He has been for us, His answers to our perplexing questions begin to flow and serendipities in our unresolved problem begin to happen.

The Lord responds with His guidance for our confession, *homologeo*, "to say after." Then as a result of His leading, we make our confession of anything that stands between the Lord and us or between us and anyone else. The Lord gives us the assurance of absolution. We respond with thanksgiving.

Now we are ready for silence. It is in this silence that the Lord guides what we are to ask in our intercession for our congregation and for ourselves as their leader. Intercessory prayer for the people to whom we preach forges a bond with them. John Henry Jowett was on target: "We must bleed to bless." That quality of intercessory prayer for our listeners takes time and energy. It's worth it. To plead before God for our people actually transforms our ministry to them. Pray for those on your heart whom you sense need the message you are to preach the forthcoming Sunday. Picture the congregation assembled for worship. Focus on their response under the sway of the Holy Spirit.

Now ask the Lord how you are to pray for yourself. What would He tell you about your preaching? Pray for a fresh anointing of the superlative "glory to glory" presence and power of the Lord (2 Corinthians 3:18).

Picture your face, your countenance, your demeanor, and your enthusiasm for your exposition, your boldness, your empathy—yes, your passion for Christ and for preaching. Hold the picture. We all are becoming what we dare to envisage. Without a vision—we perish in mediocrity and our people perish in a muddle.

The final part of our personal dialogical prayer is commitment. I like to think of the two-dimensional commitment Paul talks about in the first chapter of his second letter to Timothy, written from prison before his death. Starting in verse nine Paul reminds the young leader of who he is, to Whom he belongs, and for what he was destined. These are astounding assurances we need as much as Timothy. Timothy was singled out to receive grace and a holy calling to communicate Christ, he had experienced the new life he offered to others, and for that he was entrusted with the gospel, the good news of Christ's life, cross, resurrection, and reigning power.

To respond, Timothy needed to make a commitment. As a reminder, Paul declared the assurance of his commitment of his own life to the Lord: "I know whom I have believed and am persuaded that He is able to keep what I have committed to Him until that Day" (2 Timothy 1:12). Then he encouraged Timothy to accept and use what had been entrusted to him: "That good thing which was committed to you, keep by the Holy Spirit who dwells in us" (verse 14). Timothy was to learn from the apostle the true meaning of an unreserved commitment, and in turn, his commitment was to keep what was committed to him.

Think of that in the context of our preaching. There are two aspects of our dual commitment to preach: the calling committed to us and our commitment of our privilege of preaching. Day by day; week by week; all of our lives!

The Greek word translated as "committed" is *paratheke*. It literally means a deposit entrusted to another person's care for safekeeping. There were no banks in Paul's time, so it was a very important duty to accept the responsibility for another person's valuables. An equally high trust was to ask a person to invest your money for you and return to you the interest earned. The Greek word for "keep," *phulaxai,* meant to guard the valuables against robbery or loss.

The words "committed" and "keep" are linked closely together in both verse 12 and 14. Paul unreservedly had committed his total life to Christ. Beyond any doubt, he trusted Christ completely. He knew Him personally, he had experienced His power and unswerving reliability, and he trusted that He was able to multiply his effectiveness in his ministry. In that context, the apostle said to Timothy, in essence, "The life-changing ministry entrusted to you, multiply it with the power of the Holy Spirit who dwells in you."

Every day for 60 years that I've gone into my study for my personal prayer time and then preparation for sermons I am to preach, I have begun on my knees. The gift of preaching has been committed to me and I must consistently commit it to the Lord. When I do make this commitment each day, the Lord entrusts back to me the gift and fellowship with Him, the Giver, along with the power to discern and do His will. He reassures me of His faithfulness, guidance, and something else—without which I could not prepare to preach—the supernaturally endowed ability to plumb the depths of the Scriptures and communicate them to twenty-first-century believers and nonbelievers who need Christ more than their next breath and without Whom they will be lost now and for eternity.

For me it is a tremendous relief to know that it is by the Lord's call that I am privileged to preach. I'm sure you feel the same. To recap: The Lord has committed to us the responsibility, and we respond by committing back to Him what He has committed to us.

Here is a motto for us: "Commit your way [preaching] to the LORD, trust also in Him, and He shall bring it [with supernatural power and passion] to pass...Rest in the LORD, and wait patiently for Him" (Psalm 37:5,7).

> The Lord has committed to us the responsibility, and we respond by committing back to Him what He has committed to us.

When I was chaplain of the United States Senate, I had an experience that I will never forget. It reaffirmed my commitment to pray for the senators whom I was privileged to serve, much as I had prayed for the leaders and members of the congregations where I had been pastor.

I made up a list of the 100 senators, divided into 5 groups of 20. Each morning, Monday through Friday, I would get up at 5:30 a.m. and walk over to the Capitol, just ten minutes from my home. Then I would walk around the Capitol repeatedly while praying intently for 20 senators and their families each day. No one knew what I was doing until I published copies of my prayer list and gave one to each of the senators, asking them to join me in prayer for each other every morning.

Late one morning, I was walking down a corridor of the Russell Building on my way to a meeting. Suddenly, I met a senator whom I would have least expected to be enthusiastic about having prayers prayed for him personally.

To my surprise, he was waving his copy of my prayer list and shouting, "Chaplain, Chaplain! This is my day!" He had noted that his name was among the 20 prayed for that day. He was having a great day with some unexpected serendipities. A friendship was formed between the two of us that morning that later led to a profound, life-changing commitment of his life to Christ.

There's an old shibboleth that says, "Prayer changes things!" When it comes to preaching, it changes the preacher into a passionate communicator, and then transforms the people to whom he or she preaches.

Passionate preachers pray!

Chapter 5

The Parish of the Preacher

Before we get into the actual preparation and presentation of the sermon, we need to think together about a fresh vision of the purpose of the parishes in which we are called to preach. It is no less than the chief end of humankind, as declared in the answer to the first question in the Westminster Catechism: to glorify God and *enjoy* Him forever.

Paul declares this purpose in a doxology in Ephesians 3:21: "To Him be glory in the church by Christ Jesus to all generations, forever and ever. Amen."

Our churches exist to be the fellowship in which the Father is glorified. But note who does the glorifying. The New King James Version renders this verse in a way that suggests that it is Christ who glorifies the Father in the church.

Christ is in His church to glorify the Father through us. As we have noted, *glory* means both manifestation and adoration. We behold glory and we give glory, and Christ enables us to do both. He is the Father's manifestation with us and in us, and the One who motivates our praise. The Lord of the church is at the same time the glory from the Father in the church and the Glorifier of the Father through the church. This is a stirring thought for our churches. It also helps us articulate a clear vision of what the church was meant to be.

Churches, like individuals, become what they envision. Our churches move toward the image and goals Christ enables us to dream. We can move from what we are to what we are destined to be only if we see our churches through Christ's eyes. Then we set our priorities and reorder our life in our parishes to effectively achieve what He created them to accomplish.

Christ calls our churches to join Him in glorifying the Father. Everything we do, say, plan, program, budget, and organize must work together for this ultimate purpose.

You may have sighed to yourself, "Meanwhile, Lloyd, get back to reality, get back to the real world, get back into the church as I know it. What you're saying is lovely but you're not talking about the church today. That's so far from what my parish is that I don't even know where to begin to grapple with what you've said."

A recent report from the Pew Forum on Religion and Public Life seems to confirm the diminishing enthusiasm for the local church in America:

> Protestants now make up 48 percent of Americans, compared with nearly two-thirds in the 1970s. The decline is concentrated in the mainline denominations. Two-thirds of the unaffiliated say they still believe in God, but they overwhelmingly express disenchantment with religious organizations for being too concerned with politics within the church, tradition, money, power, and irrelevancy to the challenges of life in these tough times. The trend toward dropping away from mainline churches is evident across gender, income, and educational levels. A third of adults under thirty have no affiliation, compared with just 9 percent among those 65 and older.[4]

In the light of these grim statistics, we need a fresh vision for the parish church and need to become leaders in a counterculture renewal of the church in America. To begin we must grapple with this awesome purpose of the church as Paul has stated it so clearly. There's been enough criticism of the church from within and without, and my intention in this chapter is not to add to it.

Rather, we need a positive picture of what could happen in our churches if they were to allow Christ to be our glory and our instigation and inspiration for glorifying and enjoying the Father together.

The Positive Picture

Over the years, this picture of a local congregation in our time has been etched in my mind. I've tried to live the vision in the churches I've served together with adventuresome church officers and members. We've studied the Scriptures, prayed, and dreamed together. Then we've tried to structure the life of the parish according to the goals and priorities the Lord has revealed.

There are four inventory questions I have asked of myself and church officers of the congregations I have served:

1. What kind of people do we want to deploy in the world?

2. What kind of church equips that kind of people?

3. What kind of church officers enable that kind of church?

4. What kind of pastor or pastors enliven that kind of church officers?

1. What Kind of People?

The first question, "What kind of people do we want to deploy in the world?" is asked out of the biblical context that the church exists not for itself but for people outside it and the society in which it is placed. The church reaches out by creative evangelism and prophetic mission through the laity. We do not need to send people out into the world. They are there already. The challenge is to help them accept their calling and become effective.

To be in Christ is to be in ministry. We all are called to be ministers. I never use the term *minister* for myself or the clergy of the churches I have served. All of Christ's people are ministers. We are all His servants in relationships, at work, and in society. There should never be a question whether anyone who believes in Christ is a minister. The question is: What kind of minister and to what extent are we, pastors and people, living out Christ's calling? There are four qualities, irreducible ingredients, of dynamic Christianity:

- A life-affirming, transforming experience of Christ's love, forgiveness, and power with an unreserved commitment to Him.

- An infilling of His Spirit and a life that reveals His character in the fruit of the Spirit—love, joy, peace, patience, kindness, goodness, faithfulness, gentleness, self-control—and the gifts of the Spirit, particularly faith, wisdom, knowledge, discernment, prayer, healing, and servanthood.

- An accepted call into the ministry of evangelism—loving, listening, serving, caring for individuals, with a readiness to share new life and introduce people to Christ.

- A specific involvement in mission in one of the sores of suffering in our society.

Is this too much to ask of contemporary Christians in most congregations? Not at all. I think the problem is that we have expected far too little. In fact, when people are affirmed, they will rise to unprecedented heights because they know what's expected of them and are helped to reach these new heights.

As leaders we absolutely need to be clear about what we expect for our people based on a vivid picture of the quality of people Christ is seeking to produce. This image provides us with clear goals and priorities. We can picture joyous, liberated, loving, courageous, servant people. We can claim this from Christ, pray persistently for it, and work toward it. Essentially, Christ wants a laity through whom He can glorify the Father and extend His kingdom in the world.

2. What Kind of Church?

What kind of church makes possible this kind of person? How can we pray and plan for Christ's glory in the church? As I have prayed with lay leaders of churches I have served for the answer to these questions we have found it helpful to think of Christ's glory communicated through a quadrilateral church. The biblical calling of the church is

- a worshipping congregation
- a healing community
- an equipping center
- a deployment commission

I found it helpful to reorganize our church leaders into departments to both fulfill these purposes of the church and to give congruity between function and form. In each department, I have seen church leaders prayerfully seek the mind of Christ as to how He wants to glorify the Father through all the functions of His body. It is crucial to remember what kind of people He wants us to place in the world, and what will best prepare them for their ministry. I took prolonged retreats with the leaders to set short- and long-range goals that reflect Christ's answers to these questions for the church's life.

The Worshipping Congregation

As a worshipping congregation, the saints (pastor and members) gather around Christ to glorify the Father through worship inspired and guided by Him. It is liberating to sense His presence as He glorifies the Father through us as we sing praise, either led by the choir or in congregational singing.

Since confession means "to say after," we allow Christ to help us confess those things that stand between us and the Father. Then He reminds us of Calvary and His substitutionary sacrifice. It is with awe and wonder, mixed with profound joy, that as a priest among the priesthood of all believers I am privileged to articulate His own words of forgiveness and absolution.

Thanksgiving for Christ's forgiveness following confession breaks forth in joyous response. Then, with Christ in the midst of our worship, we pray our prayers of intercession and supplication in the power of His name, the name that reaches the Father's heart and conquers the forces of evil. Our corporate prayers of dedication are for the ministry of each member and for our witness together as a congregation.

> **Refocusing the purpose of worship has led me to a renewed understanding of the role of preaching.**

Refocusing the purpose of worship has led me to a renewed understanding of the role of preaching. I have taken Romans 15:29 as my guide. Writing to the Christians in Rome, Paul said, "I know that when I come to you, I shall come in the fullness of the blessing of the gospel of Christ."

"Quadraphonic Preaching"

When you and I preach, we are to come to people with the gospel of Christ. The gospel is His life, message, and power for all of our existence. We approach life's problems with the assurance of His blessing—the strength and courage to live amid the pressures, suffering, and frustrations of contemporary life. And the fullness of Christ's indwelling Spirit is the secret of living the exhilarating call to discipleship.

I call this "quadraphonic preaching." Namely, I believe that 1) the Bible is the inspired, authoritative Word of God; 2) Christ is the center of the proclamation of redemption, conversion, and new life; 3) the plumb line of the gospel is lowered to establish our call to justice and social responsibility; and 4) the baptism and repeated infilling of the Holy Spirit is essential for an empowered life. Christ is the Baptizer who baptizes us with the Holy Spirit (see Acts 2:33).

I believe Christ is calling us to biblical, evangelical, socially responsible, Spirit-filled preaching. My hope has been that on any Sunday, people could receive what they would find in a Bible church, an evangelical church, a social-action church, a charismatic church, and a good liturgical church—all rolled into one; the whole gospel for all the people.

Prayerful reevaluation of the church as a worshiping congregation has enabled me to sense where people are as they come to worship and where Christ wants them to be by the conclusion of the service.

Fostering Worship

The local church is called to minister to four groups: the outside-outsiders, who are outside of Christ and outside of fellowship; the inside-outsiders, who are inside of Christ but have not yet made a commitment to be part of the body of Christ; the outsider-insiders, religious people in the membership who need a transforming experience of Christ and an infilling of the Spirit; and the insider-insiders, who are both in Christ and in the church, but who need encouragement and training to live with boldness and courage. We cannot feed the hungry in all four groups without a consistent exposition of the Scriptures that weekly presents the "fullness of the blessing of the gospel of Christ."

I have found that it's the predictable sameness that often makes worship dull and bland. Christ is the same yesterday, today, and forever, but the many ways He leads us to glorify with gladness are constantly invigorated by His fresh inspiration.

In leading worship I keep three sayings before me. I've mentioned two earlier. One is the urgent appeal of the Greeks to Philip in Jerusalem during the last days of Jesus' ministry, "Sir, we want to see Jesus!" The second is Richard Baxter's reminder, "I preach as a dying man to dying men and women as if never to preach again." And third, on the door leading from the robing room into the sanctuary, the words, "In the name of Jesus, put the arms of your heart around the congregation."

All three exhortations infuse great enthusiasm into the opening call to worship, "The Living Christ is here! Let us glorify and enjoy God together!"

The Healing Community

The church is also called to be a healing community. Salvation brings healing and wholeness in the basic relationships of our life—with God; with ourselves, within our minds, emotions, and bodies; with others; and with our world. Christ is our Healer. He seeks to glorify the Father by mediating His power of healing for our spiritual, psychological, physical, and interpersonal needs.

Several years ago, the lay elders of the Hollywood church sought the guidance of Christ for a healing ministry. We were convinced that Christ desires to do through the church today what He did through the apostles in the book of Acts. The spiritual gift of praying for healing is for now as much as it was for then.

Throughout those years, we were convinced of our calling to pray for healing in one another's lives as a natural part of the life of our congregation. This happened informally two by two as we shared needs in classes; before, during, and after meetings; and on the phone and whenever a distress signal is given by one of the members. In addition, we had other expressions of the healing ministry of the church.

At the conclusion of our worship services, an invitation was given for people to come forward to the front of the sanctuary to kneel and pray with the elders. This was a part of the dedication portion of the worship service before the benediction, and often it continued long afterward.

The invitation was for people to receive Christ as Savior and Lord, unite with the church, or to pray for the healing of needs. Each week people streamed forward to commit their hurts and hopes to Christ and claim His healing power. Lives were changed, miracles happened, and people were set free of their anxiety and the burden of carrying their problems alone.

While we prayed for specific healing of needs, we also prayed and affirmed the healing professions. Some of the elders in the prayer ministry were physicians, psychologists, and psychiatrists.

Another healing focus was within the small-group program. We were encouraged to cluster together throughout the community in groups of no more than 12. The purpose of these groups was to study the Bible, share needs, and pray for one another. There were groups of singles, couples, teenagers, college and young adults, as well as special groups for business, entertainment, and professional people.

Also, a crucial expression of the healing ministry was through the work of our Care and Counseling Department, which provided pastoral counseling and training of lay counselors. We also had a "Creative Counseling Center" staffed by a psychiatrist and several psychologists to help meet the more intricate needs within the congregation.

The Equipping Center

In Ephesians 4:12 Paul declares that the leadership of the church is appointed "for the equipping of the saints for the work of ministry, for the edifying of the body of Christ." The church is called to be an equipping center for training every member for his or her ministry of living out the faith, personal witness and evangelism, and specific mission to heal human suffering.

The church as an equipping center involved both inquirers' groups for training new Christians and candidates for membership and the ongoing program of classes to equip people for their ministries. I like to think of the church as a seminary for lay ministers.

I was profoundly moved each time our elders met with an inquirers' group of candidates for membership. Many were new Christians, some were reaffirming their faith, and others were transferring their membership. The exciting thing to me was the variety of types of people and the unique way Christ worked in their lives—loving them, transforming them into new people, and conscripting them into the ministry of the laity. After ten weeks of training, they appeared before the session—the body of ruling elders—to share what Christ means to them, the facet of the church's equipping program in which they intended to be involved, and the focus of their ministry.

Everything we do in the church should be a part of the total equipping program. However, it is in the church-school classes, weekday courses, retreats, and conferences that the comprehensive training for ministry is accomplished. We need to keep before us the kind of people we want to deploy in the world, and this helps us set the direction of the curriculum. Our goal should be their spiritual formation through study of the Scriptures, prayer, theology, the ethics of holy living, and practical training in the skills of lay ministry.

The glory of Christ is a person filled with the Holy Spirit and engaged in evangelism and mission. The role of the church is to launch people in their particular area of calling.

The Deployment Commission

When a church deploys, or commissions, someone, we send that person on an assignment. A missions and deployment department, besides guiding the financial giving to local, national, and world mission programs, actively evaluates the needs of the community and deploys the members in active ministry in those needs.

An ebb and flow takes place within a church as we deploy members. People are encouraged to find the need Christ wants them to fill, and then it is our responsibility to help them find others who share that concern. In the Hollywood church we formed a task force to study the problems, then moved toward action and provided mutual support for one another. Sometimes other needs were defined by the mission and deployment department staff, who formed task forces and recruited members to fill each task force. These task forces confronted the various needs in our community, such as hunger, the homeless, runaway children from all over the nation who gravitate to Hollywood, pornography, abuse of women and children, substance abuse, the "City-Dweller" program ministering to community youth and family needs, AIDS, catastrophic illness, and the complicated issues of abortion.

The exciting thing is that there's no limit to either the number or different directions such mission task forces can take.

3. What Kind of Church Officers?

Now we are ready to consider the kind of church officers needed to enable this kind of church. I think of the session, made up of all the elders, as a church in miniature. (I'll leave it to you to change the name to that of the key officers in your church—whoever is responsible to shape the goals and program of the parish under the guidance of Christ, the Glorifier in the church.) I believe that the quality of life experienced by these lay leaders directly determines the spiritual dynamism of a church as a whole. I think of it this way: a local church will move forward only as fast and far as the elders have experienced Christ's glory together.

Some spiritual laws must be at work in and among the lay leaders: Nothing can happen *through* us which has not happened *to* us; we can reproduce only what we are in the process of rediscovering for ourselves; and our own spiritual growth determines the extent to which we can help others mature.

It is crucial to elect leaders who are vitally alive in Christ, are growing in discipleship, and are wide open to His supernatural power to lead a supernatural church. They must be people who are secure in their sainthood, filled with the Spirit, equipped with the gifts of the Spirit, and free in the Spirit. *There must be undeniable evidence that these leaders enjoy and glorify God.* To state the obvious, if we want to deploy in the world people who are biblically rooted, Christ-centered, Spirit-empowered, evangelism-motivated, and missions-oriented, then we need lay leaders who are active in ministry themselves.

A good question to ask is, "If the whole church were a projection of the spirituality of a candidate for church leadership, what kind of church would it be?" Likewise, church leaders need to ask themselves the same question: "What is my boldest dream for my church? Am I living what I long for the whole church to be?"

Equally important is how they perceive the quality of their life together as a team of leaders. If the leadership group is only a board to weigh facts and set policies, then the church is in trouble. The church officers are meant to be the beloved community gathered around Christ and to be to each other His love, forgiveness, vision, and hope. This commitment requires as much time in prayer and fellowship as is spent doing the business of the church. Leaders must be a tightly knit, unified body of believers whose sole goal is to discover Christ's maximum plan for a parish, to live that in miniature together, and then to communicate this vision to the whole congregation.

Let's look at some basic examples. Every Christian should be reproductive—are the officers leading people to Christ? No Christian should be without a mission—are the officers personally in mission? Tithing is the absolute minimum, biblical standard for giving—do the officers exemplify this biblical mandate? When they are this kind of disciples, there will be no limit to how Christ will glorify the Father in a church.

To begin this adventure in our churches, we need to start from where we are. Making a start requires a clear focus of what the church is called to be and do, which takes honesty, humility, and a commitment to live our lives and lead our churches according to Christ's mandate and by His supernatural power. So...

4. What Kind of Pastor?

The pastor is pivotal. He or she is the one called by Christ to preach what He has done, to prophesy what He has promised to do, to communicate personally what He is ready to do, and to program under His guidance so that it will be done.

Tall order for a pastor? Yes, but the pastor is not called to do it alone.

Christ is the Senior Shepherd. He is Lord of the church. And He is ready to use pastors who will put Him first in their lives and allow Him to use them as channels for the flow of His vision. The pastor is not the hope of the church but the one whose primary calling is to spend the time required in studying the Scriptures and prayer until the vision flames in his or her mind and heart to enable a congregation of hopeful thinkers. This personal time with the Lord must be in addition to time spent in preparation to preach. We'll talk about that in subsequent chapters.

Prophetic preaching is strategic in the renewal of the church. Prophecy is vividly forth-telling the truth. Forcefully, irresistibly, winsomely. If there's no fire in the pulpit there's little chance of the church being on fire. The great need for the church is for biblical exposition that's both revelational and relational. The Scriptures must be explained, but also illustrated with contemporary stories about how the truth can be lived today.

> The vision proclaimed from the pulpit must be grappled with and talked through. The Lord wants an adventuresome band of friends through whom He can impart the vision.

There also needs to be that moment in every message when the preacher leans into conversation and with one-to-one intensity says, "Allow me to share what this means to me personally." Then the personal joy, excitement, pain, and vulnerability thunder through. It is from the pulpit that the fourfold calling of every Christian and the fourfold purpose of the church must be communicated.

It's in the pastoral role that the personal relationships with church officers are developed into friendships. One to one and in small clusters, the vision proclaimed from the pulpit must be grappled with and talked through. The Lord wants an adventuresome band of friends through whom He can impart the vision. Since a church will move no faster or further than the lay leaders are living individually and together, the pastor must begin with them and never let up.

In the ambience of affirmation, trust, and openness the session, consistory, or official board or vestry becomes a fellowship of friends, covenant brothers and sisters with whom the inventory questions about where the church is going can be asked and answered together.

The role of the pastor as programmer is also strategic. Christ *does* equip leaders with gifts to be strategists. But we've all learned repeatedly that people can support only what they've shared in envisioning and developing. So, the pastor is one of a team of leaders who seek Christ's guidance in five-, three-, and one-year plans. Through His guidance, new programs are hammered out until everyone agrees to them and commits to them. Papers on a congregation's stand on issues must be written so the officers can support a particular direction. And like a family that feels the strength of a mother and father who are of one mind, so too a congregation will sense the impact of unified direction from the church officers.

One further word about pastors who foster glory in the church. Most of them have a covenant group outside their churches to which, on a regular basis, they can go to receive healing and renewed strength. The demands of leading a parish are enervating, with great potential for disappointment and discouragement, and the very real possibility of physical and spiritual burnout. The pastor needs a place where he or she can go while bruised and bleeding, exhausted and depleted, and be listened to and prayed for. Within this covenant group the pastor's vision can be recaptured and new hope engendered.

Christ is not finished with His church. It's His chosen instrument on earth through which He intends to glorify the Father. We are uniquely called, distinctly different, and sublimely blessed to be the church, those who "enjoy Him forever."

"To God be glory in the church by Christ Jesus throughout all ages, world without end. Amen."[5]

Chapter 6

The Preparation of the Preacher

Now we are ready to move on to one of the most vital factors of preaching with passion: *We must be committed to be thorough in preparation.*

Our passion, *pathein,* should be focused in *spoudé,* diligence, earnestness, and intentionality. There is no alternative. Great preaching is the result of one hour of specific preparation for each minute in the pulpit delivering the sermon!

John Henry Jowett said,

> Preaching that costs nothing accomplishes nothing. If the study is a lounge, the pulpit will be impertinence...I must put my best into my preparations, and then the Lord will honor my work. My part is to be of "pure gold" if my God is to dwell in it. I must not satisfy myself with cheap flimsy and then assume that the Lord will be satisfied with it. He demands my very best as a condition of His enriching presence....Let me present to Him pure gold. Let me offer Him nothing cheap.[6]

Donald Barnhouse put it this way: "If I knew the Lord was coming in three years, I would spend two years studying and one year preaching."

Listening

For me, a most valuable lesson about preparation that I have learned is the importance of listening to people in profound, caring relationships.

The preacher's listening moves back and forth between listening to God and listening to the people to whom he or she preaches.

When we listen attentively to our people, we discover their hurts and hopes, their deepest questions, and their most urgent needs. There is nothing so foolish as the answer to an unasked question. The problem with many preachers is that they insist on answering theoretical questions that may not have occurred to their people. Conversely, there is nothing so powerful as a biblical exposition that is Christ-centered, Holy Spirit–empowered, passionate, personal, empathetic, and illustrated from real life today.

Over the years in the parish I was led to develop broader methods of surveying the needs and questions of my congregations and radio and television audiences. "What are your most urgent questions and your deepest needs?" I asked repeatedly.

I would read the responses carefully and categorize them and then put them into a footlocker that I eventually would take with me on my study leave in Scotland each summer.

The trunk became very heavy through the year. When the bellmen of my hotel carried it up the stairs, they would mutter, "Ach, Dr. Ogilvie 'as got a dead body in this trunk!" Actually, it was filled with very urgent expressions of need from living people whom I hoped would be more alive than ever by meeting Christ or more excited about life by becoming His disciples.

The first week of my time away was spent prayerfully rereading each person's expression of need. I would hold each letter, note card, or slip of paper people had sent me or had been collected from them in worship services or handed to me personally. As I did, I felt the Lord pressing next to my heart each person who had written.

Only after that long process did I turn to the Scriptures and ask the Lord to guide me to passages particularly suited for the expositions dealing with these needs or questions, which I would include in the sermon schedule for the program year ahead. Added to these were themes the

Lord had put on my mind and heart from sensitivity to the crises and the justice issues during that current year.

Often in my devotional reading of the Bible during the year before the study leave, verses or passages would leap off the page demanding to be preached. I kept a notebook in which I listed these as the basis of prospective sermons. It is important to remember that selecting texts should not be limited only to responses to people's expressions of needs and questions. The Lord knows the needs of our people better than we do and asks us to listen to Him as He seeks to care for them through our preaching. It is the back-and-forth, combined listening to the Lord and to our people that is most effective. "This is what people are asking" must always be bonded to "Thus says the Lord" biblical exposition.

I followed the major divisions of the church year with special expositions planned for the seasons of the Christian calendar and the key Sundays of each season. This assured a careful reemphasis on the central themes of the *kerygma* and *didache*. I found it helpful to develop a preaching guide including the title, text, outline, and explanation of all of the messages from September through June.

Then a file folder was tagged for each sermon. Soon each folder was filled with Scriptural references, quotes, and notes collected during my study leave and throughout the months prior to the week a particular sermon was to be constructed for the following Sunday.

Once a biblical text was selected, I then exegeted it from the original Greek or Hebrew, gleaning and writing down etymological insights that opened the meaning for the exposition. The strongest and most helpful preaching expounds a text or passage in dynamic relationship to its actual setting in Scripture. Loyalty to the Word of God demands in-depth care in exegesis.

Employing Resources

The next step in preparation for me was to draw on the basic resource of my own personal, firsthand experience with the content of the biblical text. I made notes on what the text meant to me personally and on the fresh insights the Lord gave me as I studied. Then I recorded the problems of people's lives, the conditions with which they were grappling, and how the text spoke to these needs and gave inspiration and guidance for these struggles or affirmation of people's commitment and longing to grow in their faith.

My part was to be alert and sensitive to people's difficulties, aspirations, conflicts, frustrations, to their social and economic strains and stresses, to their insecurities, to their dreams and defeats, victories and tragic mistakes.

I have found that firsthand grappling with contemporary issues in the world, a working knowledge of psychology and sociology, and practical experience of living in fellowship and friendship with our people brings an indispensable contribution to the resources of insight, understanding, and empathy out of which we are prepared to preach with passion.

Another crucial part of our weekly preparation of sermons is our reading of insightful commentaries, great theologians, and biblical preachers of the centuries. I firmly believe that the preacher must study, study, and study! The most pitiful figure is a preacher who has stopped growing intellectually and spiritually.

William Barclay, New Testament scholar and preacher at Trinity College, University of Glasgow, once said about the preacher's need to keep reading,

> He will be in constant touch with minds far greater than his own. A preacher without a library is like a workman with no tools. The preacher who ceases to read will also cease to preach in any real sense of the term. He is a bold man who thinks that he can afford to neglect what the great minds of the past and of the present have left to him. Perhaps the decline in preaching is due to the fact that so many of us spend too much time at committees and too little time in our studies.

As a part of my weekly study, I found it very helpful to read how outstanding scholars and preachers had dealt with the passage on which I was working. The volumes of *20 Centuries of Great Preaching* published by Word Inc. some years ago were very helpful. And always it was an inspiration to read preachers like C.H. Spurgeon, G. Campbell Morgan, Alexander Maclaren, J.H. Jowett, Arthur John Gossip, Martyn Lloyd-Jones, Donald and John Ballie, Billy Graham, John Stott and, of course, James Stewart and Thomas Torrance, whom I have previously mentioned. Some of my contemporary favorites are Richard Mouw, Mark Labberton, Craig Barnes, David Fergusson, Ken Ulmer, Jack Hayford, Stewart Briscoe, James Earl Massey, and so many more friends.

Determining Parts, Points, and Progression

After all my preliminary preparation, I was ready to determine the introduction, body of thought, and closing of the sermon. I also spent a great deal of time thinking through the progression of the major points of the body of thought. When these elements were firmly in my mind, I was ready to write out an outline.

The basic goal of the sermon was written at the top of the page. I forced myself to answer these questions: "What is the aim and intention of this sermon? What is the central truth it is to convey? Can I concentrate that into a single sentence?" Beneath the goal, the crucial idea of the introduction is clearly stated. The body of thought is enumerated under main headings and then the thrust of the call for a response in the closing.

J.H. Jowett said,

> I have a conviction that no sermon is ready for preaching until we can express its theme in a short, pregnant sentence as clear as crystal. I find the getting of that sentence is the hardest, the most exacting, and the most fruitful labour in my study. I do not think that any sermon ought to be preached, or even written, until that sentence has emerged, clear and lucid as a cloudless moon.[7]

Following Jowett's advice and with all my preparation completed, I am ready to write the sermon. I'm convinced that writing out sermons is an absolutely necessary discipline to clarify my thoughts definitively, and also is a way to avoid muddled thinking, pet phrases, jargon, and clichés. Writing the sermon safeguards against shallowness, simplicity, and sloppiness. Also, it defends our listeners from extemporaneous wanderings in which we aim at nothing and hit it!

I am fully aware of the current popularity of ad-lib sermons. In addition to more informal orders of worship, music, and casual attire, there is a growing demand for preachers to look and sound like they are preaching "off the cuff" or under the immediate inspiration of the Holy Spirit without prior preparation. The danger is when we use this as an evasion for hours of study. In fact, thorough preparation is the only way we can speak with great freedom and joy and also sound like we've had hours in prayer and study under the guidance of the Holy Spirit.

There's a wonderful story about when Martin Luther decided to test the Holy Spirit's power by going into the pulpit to preach extemporaneously without his customary study of the biblical text. He told his friend Melanchthon that the Holy Spirit spoke to him as he preached. "What did He say?" Melanchthon asked. Luther replied, "He said, 'Martin, you are not prepared!'"

So that the Holy Spirit never need say that to us, in the next chapters I want to share further discoveries I have made about the development of the introduction, body of thought, and closing of the sermon of a passionate preacher. First, let's talk about the introduction—what, as a fisher of men and women, I like to call "the setting of the hook."

Chapter 7

Three Minutes to Set the Hook

In this cybernetic age the first three minutes of the sermon are for "setting the hook." Whether we preach twenty minutes, thirty minutes, or more, during these three minutes we will either win or lose our listeners. What we write on the first two pages of a fifteen-page manuscript is crucial to prepare us to open the sermon with strength and confidence.

In the introduction we can establish in words and attitude our empathy and caring, and how the sermon is going to make a difference in people's lives. However, sometimes I experienced frustration in getting started with the introduction. Ever have that problem?

Ernest Hemingway said that his most anguishing hours as a writer were spent deciding how to begin a novel. After he had developed the plot, the story line, and the main and supporting characters, he would sit with a blank page before him wondering how to start in a way that would grip his readers. Finally, he would sit in front of the fireplace with an orange and let the peelings drop into the fire. As the blue flames sputtered and flickered, Hemingway tried to focus on the one thing he wanted to communicate. When that was clear, the opening paragraphs formed in his mind; and he was ready to return to his desk and fill in the blank page—and hundreds of pages after that.

> The most effective introduction to the sermon came...as the gift of the Holy Spirit, coupled with a lot of hard work, a profound love for my listeners, and a longing to communicate with them.

As preachers, we certainly can empathize with Hemingway's difficulty getting started. I can remember many times sitting at my desk with everything in the outline completed except the introduction. The sermon had been planned the summer before while on my study leave. Ideas and illustrations had been gathered in subsequent months. The first part of the week had been spent on in-depth research and exposition of the biblical text. Now it was time to write the sermon. How should I begin?

Sometimes, I would have to wait, pray, and pace the floor until the most effective introduction to the sermon came. And when it did, I knew it was the gift of the Holy Spirit, coupled with a lot of hard work, a profound love for my listeners, and a longing to communicate with them.

The Basics of the Introduction

I have discovered that the most effective introductions are written out after the outline of the sermon has been completed. During my research for a sermon, I have three sets of paper handy: one for the introduction, one for the body of thought, and another for the conclusion.

On the introduction page, under Roman numeral "I," I put "A—Statement of the purpose of the sermon." Then under "B," I list out the illustrations, stories, or anecdotes that may be useful in writing the introduction, remembering that variety is a virtue for introductions. Under "C," I write out how the sermon will help people live life to the fullest now and forever.

The purpose statement, "A" of the outline of the introduction, is strategic and of primary importance. Leslie D. Weatherhead, for years distinguished preacher of the historic City Temple in London, said,

> It is my practice, when I am trying to make a sermon, to write out at the head of a sheet of paper the aim of the sermon—what I hope the sermon will achieve. It is a good thing for a preacher to

> keep that in mind lest he preach a sermon of interest, and per-
> haps, usefulness to himself, but to very few others. Let him set
> down in black and white what he expects his discourse to do.[8]

Without that kind of clarity of purpose, the sermon will aim at nothing and hit it. The lack of a clear purpose statement will also make writing the introduction very difficult. The goal of an introduction is to
state the purpose of the message in the most effective and varied form.

It was said of Gerald Kennedy, the Methodist bishop, that he began
the sermon where you might expect him to end. He affirmed his audience in his introduction by assuming their willingness to grow and apply
the convictions they held, but which needed to be lived. He spent a
great deal of time writing his introductions. He said, "There is no room
for debate as to what the introduction ought to do. We are simply trying to get our people to want to hear what we have to say."[9]

Robert J. McCracken, distinguished pastor of Riverside Church in
New York City for many years, believed similarly. In his book *The Making of a Sermon*, he explained how important the introduction is to an
effective sermon. He would do the first draft of the sermon outline on
Tuesday. He sorted and sifted his source materials accumulated over a
period of time. Then he would begin to sketch an outline. By Wednes-
day morning he was at work on the introduction of the sermon. He said,

> Experience has taught me that may take some considerable
> time…I have written and rewritten the introduction over and
> over again. And I have discovered that once satisfied with the
> introduction, the remainder of the sermon can be done more
> rapidly. The introduction takes time because here consider-
> ations of style are especially paramount. A well-constructed
> sentence is like a sharpened tool. If the sermon opens with sen-
> tences that are concise and precise, it will arouse interest and
> it may linger in the memory. What are the requirements for a

> good introduction? It should never be lengthy. Any tendency
> to become expansive or discursive, as if all the time in the world
> were at our command, must be resisted. We ought to come to
> grips at once and forthrightly with our subject. It should be as
> interesting as we can make it.[10]

The kind of lengthy, rambling introductions that might satisfy our own need for rapport with our people, and that McCracken deplored, will not work today. We preach in a day of "media bites" by secular television communicators who have polished the art of capturing and keeping people's attention.

A parishioner described his pastor's introductions to sermons in a colorful way: "Ever see a bull at a bullfight when it is getting ready to run headlong toward the matador's red flag? It moves about nervously, sniffs and snorts, rakes the ground with its front hooves, then finally focuses on the target and goes for it with gusto. Well, our pastor is like that in the first minutes of his sermon. Once he gets going, it's pure gold, but oh, the agony of the beginning—for him and for the congregation!"

This pastor's proclivity distracts from the content of the body of the message. Chances are that he has not topped off the extensive research I know he does with a carefully prepared introduction.

This will require both writing and memorizing the introduction. Writing is the expression of refined and polished thought. Memorizing our introductions frees us to look our people in the eye and establish communication. It need not be memorized word for word, but repeated reviews of it, plus saying it out loud, will fix it in our verbal memory patterns.

Predictability is our bane and the congregation's boredom. A preacher who starts with an anecdote, three points, and a poem every Sunday deserves the "ho-hum" attitude he or she eventually receives from the congregation. To avoid this, it is good actually to keep a log of the types of introductions used and be sure they have been rotated. Here are a few types I have found most effective:

1. A personal story from my own life pilgrimage, followed by application of the biblical text and statement of the purpose of the message.

2. A real-life story that gets to the essence of what I feel called to preach and then a lead-in to the biblical text.

3. An anecdote or parable from contemporary life or history that exposes the central thrust of the biblical text. Then I state the purpose and press on with the thesis and points of the body of thought.

4. A direct statement from the biblical text and what it promises for our contemporary challenges and concerns.

5. An empathetic reference to a question or need expressed by many in the congregation and how the exposition of the biblical text offers a response. I find it electrifying to know that the message the Lord has inspired me to develop, commit to memory, and saturate with prayer is in response to many people's searching, yearning, and sometimes anguish. J.B. Phillips said that translating the book of Acts in the context of the church's need for power was like rewiring an old farmhouse with the current turned on!

6. The dramatic retelling of the story line of a biblical account or parable with "you are there" intensity. I state the essence of the timeless truth and intimate that the message is going to reveal how what God did then, He can and will do today.

7. The straightforward statement of a contemporary problem or issue and then a move into the biblical text as God's solution or mandate.

8. Asking questions that get to the core of a human need. These "Do you ever..." "Have you ever..." questions should be followed by an "of course, we all do" kind of

empathy, and then a statement of how the Lord can meet the need and how this message will help explain what He has promised in the biblical text that He is ready to do.

9. A clearly stated paragraph of the essential truth that the entire message will elucidate. Then state the points to be covered, and move on.

10. Recounting a current news item that is on people's minds, dilating the contemporary focus for the biblical text to be preached. This opens the way to show how the Bible speaks today, answers our "why" questions, and provides comfort, challenge, and courage.

In any of and all of the types of introduction to a sermon I have listed there must be a note of urgency, authority, vulnerability, or a touch of good humor. A congregation needs to know that the sermon is crucial for their lives, now and for eternity. Since we are not simply proclaiming our views but God's good news, there should be a "thus says the Lord" sense of intrepid conviction based on biblical authority.

At the same time, we need to indicate that the truth we are about to proclaim has had an impact on our own lives. Thus we do not stand over or above our people, telling them something *they* need to know that we have long since digested and are living to perfection. Rather, we stand with them as mutual recipients of what the Lord has to say through His Word.

The introduction of a particular sermon must be consistent with our purpose in preaching. The sermon is our part of an ongoing dialogue with our people. As I have stressed earlier, the sermon arises out of listening to them, and to God, in our study of the Word and in prayer. We listen to our people in conversations and counseling with sensitivity to what is going on in them, their relationships, and their struggle with the soul-sized issues of justice and righteousness in our society.

Now, let us go over some of the types of introductions and consider specific examples. As I continue to write this chapter, the actual wording of these will be set off so you can distinguish between my ongoing conversation with you the reader, and the quotation of an introduction of a sermon I preached or found in researching sermons of other preachers. Here goes!

Anecdotes and Personal Stories

An Episcopal priest went out into the chancel of a cathedral and spoke the traditional words, "The Lord be with you," to which the people were to respond "and with your spirit." Since the nave and the chancel were divided by a distance, the priest was totally dependent on the public address system. The congregation had not heard his opening words because two little wires in his microphone were disconnected. Catching the eye of a fellow priest in the chancel, he banged the microphone in his hand. As he did, the two little wires were reconnected and what he said to his fellow priest was broadcast loudly throughout the sanctuary.

"There's something wrong with this microphone!" he shouted.

And the people, in rote, patterned response said, "And with your spirit!"

This story then can be followed by something like these transitional lines:

At times all of us have something wrong with our spirits, our dispositions, and moods. I suspect you and I have a mutual problem: sometimes our dispositions contradict what we say we believe. But what do you do when you feel down or have a rotten disposition? I know from experience that trying to talk myself into a new attitude with glib thought condition-ers doesn't work. Know what I mean? I know you do. We are cut from the same cloth, you and I, when it comes to "ward-robing" the frustrations.

Often we panic, blame others or circumstances, react with fear, or pretend we've got it all together. It's then that we need grace, the grace of the Lord Jesus and His Spirit, to transform us.

Paul's final benediction in his letter to the Galatians is more than a traditional postscript. Backed up by a living Lord, it is a promise that we don't have to stay the way we feel: "May the grace of our Lord Jesus Christ be with your spirit." We are offered a grace-captivated disposition! Now let's discover what that really is, how we can receive it fresh every day, and how we can become communicators of grace.

What happened to me at a luncheon in Darien, Connecticut, is an example of a personal-story introduction that points away from our-selves and puts preacher and people in a position to receive the trans-forming power of Christ. Here's the introduction:

A woman stood up to introduce me as the speaker of a luncheon. What she said put panic in my soul. "We have someone with us today who will change our lives," she said. "He will give us hope, new self-esteem, and power to live a dynamic life!" she went on confidently. I wanted to crawl under the table as she continued: "Meeting this person will be like the rivers of your life will stop and flow in a new direc-tion. You'll experience freedom, joy, and gusto in your life."

The woman paused, smiled, and said: "This person's name is Jesus Christ…and here is Lloyd Ogilvie to tell us about Him!"

It was one of the best introductions as a speaker I've ever received. It explains why I'm alive, why I feel called to preach, and what my essential message is: Christ; Christ crucified; Christ risen and reigning; Christ indwelling as Lord!

Telling that story really works for me as the introduction to a sermon on the new creation and what it means to be a new creature in Christ. This story also prepares the way for an exposition on a text like Romans 15:29: "I know that when I come to you, I will come in the fullness of the blessing of the gospel of Christ."

In an introduction to a sermon on hope, I used my own experience of being given the gift of hope when I crushed the tibial plateau of my left knee into seven parts in a traumatic hiking accident in Scotland. The following opening paragraph set the scene and enabled me to share my own witness to God's powerful promise in Jeremiah 29:11: "I know the plans I have for you...to give you a future and a hope" (RSV). Here is how I started:

I might have died...but God had other plans. In what turned out to be one of the most traumatic episodes of my life, God gave me new excitement for the future through a dramatic experience of authentic hope.

Then I told the story of how I crawled on my back for almost three hours while the Lord kept repeating, "Crawl, Lloyd, crawl! Don't give up! I have plans for you to give you a future and a hope!"

When I finally reached a dirt road, I was rescued by a man and his two children who were taking a walk. "Who are you?" the man asked. I told him I was Lloyd Ogilvie from Los Angeles. Without missing a beat, the man asked, "You wouldn't happen to know Jeremy Swan, would you?" Out of the fog of extreme pain I responded, "Yes, I know him. He's one of my best friends. Why?"

The man smiled with pleasure. "Well, I'm a cardiologist. The great Swan is my hero in the practice of cardiology. I'll take care of you now!" (I really don't think he would have left me there writhing in pain if we hadn't had a hero and friend in common. It was late in the afternoon. I don't think I could have made it through the night crawling on the road alone.)

Jeremy Swan, the world-famous cardiologist, was the inventor of the catheter used in open-heart surgery and was a member of my church in Hollywood, a confidant in a small prayer group, and indeed, a wonderful friend. There on a dirt road in the Highlands of Scotland, a doctor who admired my friend Swan just happened to be taking a walk with his two children. Just happened? No, he was there by God's appointment. As I crawled, God had given me hope and used the confluence of a doctor's walk on a dirt road and my arrival on the road to give me confidence for the rest of my life that He provides what He promises! He follows through when He promises a future and a hope!

An introduction for another sermon on hope entitled "Where There's Hope There's Life" is as follows. As you will surmise, the doctor in this introduction was not Jeremy Swan! The introduction to this sermon went like this:

I have a good friend who is a doctor of internal medicine. He has a saying that he repeats as he leaves a patient in a hospital room. After he has checked the charts on the patient's progress, takes his or her pulse, and discusses the prognosis, just before he turns to go, he says, "Well, where there's life, there's hope!"

After that, I went on with this transition:

> What I want to say is in bold contradiction to that ambiguous prognosis. In fact, my thesis is just the opposite. I believe that where there is hope, there's life. Hope enables a quality of life. It sets us free to dare, gives us confidence in daily frustrations, and courage to live adventurously. Jesus said, "I have come that you might have life abundant." Hope is the key that opens the floodgates of His power and unlocks the flow of His amazing, unlimited possibilities. Emil Brunner was right: "What oxygen is to lungs, hope is to the soul."
>
> If you and I could sit down for a good visit, I'd want to ask you three questions. Do you have hope? Is your hope based on a source that is reliable? Are you a hopeful person who can communicate authentic, lasting hope to others? If I were to answer my own questions, I'd have to share the convictions I have about what hope is not, and what it really is. The scripture we read from 1 Peter chapter 1, particularly verses 3-6, has meant a lot to me personally: "Blessed be the God and Father of our Lord Jesus Christ, who according to His abundant mercy has begotten us again to a living hope through the resurrection of Jesus Christ from the dead…in this you greatly rejoice…"
>
> This morning I want to talk about true hope, hope that is not simply wishful thinking or yearning about the future. The resurrection breaks the seal of hopelessness and gives us a reliable, dynamic expectation for our lives in this portion of eternity and forever. True hope comes from the power of the resurrection.

These introductory words can lead to an exposition of the text and a conclusion that may include this affirmation:

For resurrection living, there's resurrection power. And oh,
the joy of living every hour. For all of life's an Eastertide for
those who, with hope, in the living Christ abide!

True Stories of Others

The use of true stories of other people can be very effective as an
introduction. The story should encapsulate the essence of the main
point and purpose of the sermon. If the account is of a contemporary
person, be sure to get permission; and if historical, be sure to get the
facts straight.

A couple allowed me to use the account of a turbulent counseling session with me before they were reconciled and began a new life
together. The account opened a sermon on Christian marriage:

> The couple sat on the couch in my study. They sat as far apart
> as the arms on the two ends of the couch would permit. The
> husband went on endlessly in a tirade about all that his wife
> refused to be for him in their marriage. The woman, feeling
> unjustly accused, sat in stony silence until she could endure
> it no longer. She leaped to her feet, walked to the other end
> of the couch, and burst out in anger: "What will it ever take
> to satisfy you?"
>
> That's the essential question, isn't it? What would it take
> to satisfy you in your marriage? Sooner or later we are forced
> to discover that only Christ can satisfy our deepest needs.
> And when He does, we are set free to serve our spouses rather
> than keep a running account of the deficits of what he or she
> has or has not done.

After this opening, I pressed on to the biblical text and a message on
what is a Christ-centered, truly satisfying marriage.

One Easter, I opened my sermon by telling about a man who had received the risen, reigning Christ as his Savior and indwelling Lord. The shocker was that he had been a church member for years and had been to 45 Easter services in his 55 years of life. His story led into the basic theme: "For resurrection living there's resurrection power."

A woman I will call Julie gave me permission to share what happened one Sunday morning. It provided a personal account of forgiveness for the opening of a message on God's indefatigable love. The introduction went something like this:

> As I greeted the congregation streaming out of the sanctuary one Sunday morning, a woman named Julie shook my hand and urgently asked if she could talk to me after I finished. I knew something was wrong. When finally I was able to talk with her, she was sobbing convulsively. I looked into her troubled face that drugs and hard living had plowed with furrows beyond her years. Her eyes were filled with pain.
>
> "Lloyd, I stumbled! Is there hope for me?" Julie sobbed. She had slipped back into her addiction in a two-day binge. Since then she had been staying away from church because she couldn't imagine that the Lord would forgive her, or that she would be accepted by her new Christian friends.
>
> Well, you be the judge. Is there hope for Julie? Or for you or me, whatever we've done or been? Is there ever a time when God gives up on us or stops loving us or refuses to offer us forgiveness?

Accounts of Historical Figures

Accounts of historical characters also provide a launching pad lift to an introduction. The sources seem endless. Excavating the treasure of these accounts comes from extensive reading in biographies and autobiographies as well as general history.

An account of Bishop Jean Massillon's funeral oration for Louis XIV gave me exactly what I needed to open a message on pride and the grace of God:

> Notre Dame Cathedral was filled to overflowing in a spectacular moment in a secular age. The glorious, proud reign of Louis XIV had ended. His casket was placed at the center of the chancel with only one large candle beside it. That's the way the king had arranged it in his will for his funeral.
>
> Massillon mounted the pulpit. The audience fell silent. He announced his text from the Vulgate, Ecclesiastes 1:16: "I spoke in heart, saying, Behold, I have become great, and have advanced in wisdom beyond all who were before me in Jerusalem."
>
> After a long pause to allow the text to have its full effect, Massillon said: "God only is great, my brethren; and above all in those last moments when He presides at the death of the kings of the earth, the more their glory and their power have shown forth, the more vanishes; then do they render homage to His greatness; God then appears all that He is, and man is no more at all that which he believed himself to be."
>
> Massillon finished his sermon and left the pulpit, walked to the casket and solitary candle. He snuffed out the candle and repeated: "God only is great!"

After a story like that, it takes only a few transitional sentences to move into the body of thought for a message on the greatness of God and our false pride!

One of the best introductions that I have ever heard for a sermon on 2 Corinthians 4:7, "We have this treasure in earthen vessels," was as follows:

An English preacher was holding meetings in Northern Ireland. He returned to his lodging and as he stepped into the room, a hand grasped the locks at the back of his head and swung him around the room in anger.

The assailant was not a member of the IRA, but the preacher's termagant, shrewish wife. The year was not in the twenty-first century, but around 1771. The woman's name was Mary, but she went by the name Molly. And her husband's name was John Wesley![11]

Our idea that our heroes and heroines had it all together is wrong. They, like all of us, hold the treasure in earthen vessels.

One summer, on study leave in Scotland, after reading thousands of responses to my survey of the needs of my congregation and my radio and television ministries, I decided that a series of messages, and eventually a book, was needed on the promises of the Covenant. The rainbow, the sign of the Covenant, became the symbol of my studies.

You can imagine my delight when I came across a little-known fact in a biography and more recent articles about George Matheson, the blind Scottish scholar and preacher of a previous generation.[12] This gave me the title and thrust of the series. Here is the way I introduced the first of the messages in the series entitled "Climbing the Rainbow." It was about the timely interventions of God in troublesome times:

It was late in the evening of June 6, 1882. The pastor of the church in Innellan on the Firth of Clyde in Scotland sat alone in the darkness of his study. No need to turn up the gaslights. He was blind.

Then 40 years old, he had emerged as one of Scotland's most brilliant preachers and compelling poets. Crowds flooded to hear him wherever he preached; prestigious churches in Edinburgh and Glasgow sought him to be their pastor; his books and poetry were read throughout the land.

On that night in June, however, the darkness that had increasingly gathered around him since childhood was matched by the inner anguish in his heart.

It had been a long day. In the morning he had attended the marriage service for one of his sisters. A mixture of happiness and pain surged in his heart. This sister had been his eyes all through his student days in college and seminary. She learned Latin, Greek, and Hebrew so she could read to him. With her assistance he had been a brilliant student, graduating with the highest honors the University of Glasgow had to award. She accompanied him as he began his ministry, writing out his dictated sermons and reading them back to him until they were fully memorized and could then be delivered with his impelling oratorical skill. What would he do without her?

After the wedding, the blind poet-preacher took a steamer from Glasgow to Innellan. "Something happened to me," he wrote later, "which caused me the most severe mental suffering."

Was it facing the demands of his life and ministry without his sister's eyes? Was it that his sister's marriage forced him to realize that he probably would never marry? Or had he endured the rejection of someone he had hoped to marry? Were there fantasies too abhorrent to relate stalking the corridors of his mind?

Perhaps it is a good thing we don't know the details: it releases us to fill in the blanks with our own brand of "mental suffering"—anxiety, worry, stress, fear, rejection, loss, grief.

What we do know is that on that night the poet sought to battle through his anguish to a new and profound experience of the love and faithfulness of God. The rainbow, the biblical sign of God's Covenant, had been a cherished image for the preacher-poet because it was one of the last things he had seen before complete blindness set in. We should not be surprised then that the image of the rainbow appeared often in his poems. The first line in one of them discloses the personal nature of the rainbow: "Jesus, rainbow of my sorrow" and "All the tears are rainbow bright when Calvary crowns the way."

And so, with the rainbow of God's Covenant love flashing in his mind, on that June night the poet felt His presence and received the courage to go on. He picked up his pen and wrote his most famous poem—and one of the best-loved poems of the ages. "The hymn was the fruit of suffering," he said. "It was the quickest bit of work I ever did in my life. I had the impression of rather having it dictated by some inward Voice than of working it out myself. I am quite sure the whole work was completed in five minutes." The first and third stanzas capture what happened that night in June.

> O love that wilt not let me go,
> I rest my weary soul in Thee;
> I give Thee back the life I owe,
> That in Thine ocean depths its flow
> May richer, fuller be.
>
> O Joy that seekest me through pain,
> I cannot close my heart to Thee;
> *I climb the rainbow through the rain,*
> And feel the promise is not vain,
> That morn shall tearless be.

The preacher-poet's name was George Matheson, who after that night went on to be one of the greatest preachers of the nineteenth century.

Some of you may think that I have misquoted the third line of the third stanza. But that's how Matheson wrote it: "I climb the rainbow through the rain."

An interesting twist. The Hymnal Committee of the Church of Scotland insisted that line be changed to "I trace the rainbow through the rain." Matheson was not happy about the change.

For him, "climbing the rainbow" meant claiming the promise of the Covenant. The blind poet remembered the magnificent rainbows he had seen in his youth. They appeared in the midst of the storm while it was still raining. This brought to mind the rainbow as a sign of God's Covenant with Noah and all perpetual generations. It reached from heaven to earth and spanned the skies. For Matheson, the rainbow was like Jacob's ladder let down from heaven for the poet's ascent to realize the glory of God in the midst of the storm of his suffering.

James Black, in a book published 54 years after Matheson's death, wrote, "It is merely silly to think of Matheson tracing that rainbow through the rain; his eyes were shut forever! But in his own fine imagination, he could picture himself stumbling forward blindly till he actually touched the rainbow with his groping fingers! And when he touched it, he could grasp it and climb it...God's rainbows are not to be traced, but climbed."[13]

I had an opening for the completed outline of a message on Noah, the first in a series on the Covenant. The phrase "climbing the rainbow" became the theme of the series and subsequently the title of a book.[14]

Another poet provided an introduction to a sermon on God's providence worded as follows:

In despair, William Cowper decided to drown himself in the Thames. He left his home and hired a horse-drawn cab to take him to the river. After hours of searching in heavy fog, the cab driver ended up at the door of Cowper's home! Cowper stumbled into his house, fell on his knees, and gave his life to God. Then he wrote what became a famous poem and hymn, "God Moves in a Mysterious Way His Wonders to Perform."

> God moves in a mysterious way
> His wonders to perform;
> He plants His footsteps in the sea
> And rides upon the storm.
>
> Deep in unfathomable mines
> Of never-failing skill,
> He treasures up His bright designs
> And works His sovereign will.
>
> Ye fearful saints, fresh courage take:
> The clouds ye so much dread
> Are filled with mercy and will break
> In blessings on your head.
>
> Judge not the Lord by feeble sense,
> But trust Him for His grace;
> Behind a frowning providence
> He hides a smiling face.
>
> His purposes will ripen fast,
> Unfolding every hour;
> The bud may have a bitter taste,
> But sweet will be the flower.

> Blind unbelief is sure to err
> And scan His work in vain;
> God is His own interpreter,
> And He will make it plain.

Subsequently, Cowper became a noted English poet and also worked closely with John Newton in publishing a book of 660 hymns.

Needs in Your Congregation

In a sermon I entitled "A Peace of Your Mind" I constructed this introduction followed by an inventory:

> "Give them a piece of your mind!" the man shouted as we passed in a hallway of the United States Capitol. He knew I was on my way to speak to a group of leaders at a crucial time of acrimonious conflict. As I walked on, it hit me: that was exactly what I wanted to do. But then the "Inner Voice" of the Holy Spirit asked, "How will you spell peace? *Piece* or *peace?*"
>
> I was reminded that the great need in the people to whom I would speak was for profound peace that would enable peacemaking. I was resolved to share the secret of lasting, liberating peace.

After I expressed my own need to receive fresh peace in my own mind repeatedly so I could help others experience peace of mind, I moved on in the introduction with an inventory of the assembled congregation about their experience of authentic peace of mind.

Sometimes, in an introduction it is helpful to involve the congregation in some kind of physical participation. In the introduction to this sermon on peace I asked people to put their right hand forward. Then I asked them to hold their thumb with their left hand and name each of the other four fingers with these words: *never, seldom, frequently, consistently*. Then I went on with the introduction:

> I want to ask you some very personal questions. Audacious? Maybe. But I if you and I had a conversation about peace, these are questions I would want you to ask me and I would want to ask you. This morning, I will answer them as honestly as I can and encourage you to do the same.
>
> In your inner self, known only to you, are you at peace? Or are you filled with a jumble of distressing memories, unresolved grievances, unfinished plans, and frustrating disappointments? Are you at peace in your thinking? Never? Seldom? Frequently? Consistently?
>
> What about your feelings? Do you feel at peace? Do you have a profound sense of serenity rooted in an unassailable security? Do you feel loved, forgiven, accepted as a unique, never-to-be-repeated miracle of God? Are you free of smoldering anger, nagging fears, and self-incrimination? Never? Seldom? Frequently? Consistently?
>
> What about the future? Are you at peace about knowing and doing God's will? Are you sure about your goals? Is your will surrendered in complete trust in the Lord? Never? Seldom? Frequently? Consistently?
>
> What about your relationships? Do you ever allow others to rob you of inner peace? Do some present relationships remind you of troubling relationships of the past? Do some people bug the heaven out of you? Are you at peace in your relationships? Never? Seldom? Frequently? Consistently?
>
> And what about circumstances? Do you remain calm in the face of trouble, crises, illness, and tough times? Do circumstances interrupt the flow of peace? Never? Seldom? Frequently? Consistently?

Finally, is your body at peace? Are you ever strained by stress, agitation, and nervousness? Are you free from tension? Churning stomach, tight muscles, and tiredness? Do you have a sense of calmness in your body? Never? Seldom? Frequently? Consistently?

I have to admit that not all my responses were "constantly" or even "frequently." But I want them to be! How about you?

Note that this inventory includes our whole being— mind, emotions, will, body, relationships, and circumstances. That's because peace is a metonym for wholeness—mental health, emotional stability, volitional integration, and physical well-being.

This is the peace Jesus Christ offers us. He promises nothing less than the same peace He had on the night before He was crucified: "Peace I leave with you, My peace I give to you; not as the world gives do I give to you. Let not your heart be troubled, neither let it be afraid" (John 14:27).

This introduction can lead into a sermon on peace as the palpable presence of Christ, the profound experience of receiving and giving forgiveness, the penetrating liberation of worries, the personal release of fears of the future, and the powerful calling of peacemaking.*

Another effective way of opening the sermon is with a personal question. This method is a bit different than the inventory I mention above. James S. Stewart was a master craftsman of many different methods of introducing the sermon, but in a sermon on the omnipotence of God, he displayed the effectiveness of questions in the introduction:

What is the biggest fact in life to you at this moment? What

---

* A full treatment of this theme is in chapter 13 of my book *Experiencing the Power of the Holy Spirit* (Harvest House Publishers, 2013).

is the real center of your universe? "The biggest fact in life?" replies one man. "Well I reckon it is my home. That for me is the center of everything." A very noble thing to say! "The main fact in life to me," says a second, "is, without a shadow of doubt, my work. If you take that away from me, you just take everything." "The central thing for me," declares a third, "is health and happiness. As long as I have that, I'm quite content. I can't bear to be unhappy." But what is your answer?

In one brief paragraph, Dr. Stewart involved the listeners and drew them into mental dialogue.

The Challenge of the Biblical Text

Another method of introducing a sermon is by quoting the biblical text and what it promises for contemporary life. Arthur John Gossip, one of the great preachers of Scotland in the 1920s, often expressed a Scot's directness by simply stating the text from the Scripture and then launching into his consistently magnificent exposition. His sermon "That Queer Complex, Human Nature" is a good example. He gave his text from Luke 3:38, "The son of Adam, the son of God," and opened by saying,

> There you have it, thrown down bluntly and vividly for all to see, the littleness and the greatness of man, that baffling self-contradiction, carried to such unbelievable lengths…that stares at and confuses all of us. A son of Adam, a mere transient nothing; earthly and of the earth; and yet a son of God, with real unquenchable spark of the divine in him! How both? Yet, is it not so we are formed, and from the jar and noisy clashing of those two opposites in us there arise all our unrest and all our glory?[15]

You can be sure that opening paragraph did not come ad lib and off the cuff. No, it was the result of polished writing and rewriting.

Congregations enjoy varied openings to sermons. After several weeks of sermons opening with stories or anecdotes, it is a welcome change for the preacher to begin by saying, "Let us get straight to the point." Then give a statement of the basic presupposition, the thesis of the message, and the biblical truth to be expounded. However, there should be a vivid illustration early on to give the people an opportunity to feel as well as conceptualize the thrust of the message.

Martyn Lloyd-Jones was the master of this method. In an evaluation of Lloyd-Jones's preaching, J.I. Packer wrote this about his introductions:

> He first announces his text, usually with some variant of the formula, "I would like to call your attention to..." The formula means just what it says. Lloyd-Jones is an expository and textual preacher and the whole concern of his sermon will be to make us attend to the message which his text contains. Next, he begins to talk around some problem of life or thought today; or some issue arising from the congregation's circumstances, or on which the text will in due course be heard to speak; or perhaps he will point to the way in which some feature of the text or context exposes and questions us today... The style of these opening minutes is conversational, informal and unstudied, yet at the same time serious and business like: You are made to feel at once that Lloyd-Jones knows exactly where he is going and that his perception of life's issues is such that he will be well worth accompanying.[16]

Another effective method of introducing the sermon is with a dramatic description of a biblical account, putting our listeners in the scene. I did a sermon entitled "Drop That Stone!" in which I described the

John 8:1-11 account of a woman caught in adultery. After a full description of the passage from inside the skins of all involved, I had four points about judgmentalism and forgiveness of others and ourselves. During the entire sermon I held a large stone, which I forcefully dropped at the end of the message while calling everyone to drop the stones of condemnation and unwillingness to forgive they had been carrying in order to stone someone who had failed.

Contemporary Problems

Often I find ideas for introductions in my reading of newspapers, magazines, novels, and contemporary biographies and autobiographies, as well as other books on social issues, psychology, and management. For example, the bestseller written a number of years ago by Tom Peters on the management revolution provides a wonderful starting place for a sermon on a biblical text that will help people handle pressure and stress. The book is entitled *Thriving on Chaos*. As Christians, we thrive *in* chaos; what a difference! From that concept, it is only a short step to quoting John 16:33 and Jesus' promise of courage in tough times.

When doing a topical sermon on a contemporary problem, it is important to state the problem clearly, show what it is doing to us, and progress to the biblical mandate. For example, in a message on pornography while I was a pastor in Hollywood, California, I opened with a statement:

> It is alarming to discover that 90 percent of the pornographic literature, magazines, films, and videos are produced within a radius of eight miles of where you are sitting in this beautiful, historic sanctuary! Today I want to confront what pornography does to pollute the American mind, its motivating influence on rape, the dehumanization of women and men, and the alarming growth of child abuse.

This was followed by illustrations and statistics and then the exposition and application of a biblical text: "This is the will of God, your sanctification: that each of you should abstain from sexual immorality; that each of you should know how to possess his own vessel in sanctification and honor, not in passion of lust, like the Gentiles who do not know God; that no one should take advantage of and defraud his brother in this matter, because the Lord is the avenger of all such, as we also forewarned you and testified. For God did not call us to uncleanness, but in holiness" (1 Thessalonians 4:3-7).

Over the years, I have found it a good rule to be sure I have a strong biblical verse or passage that confronts any social problem I preach on. The authority of the Bible as the Word of God is crucial and it is amazing to note how our problems today are dealt with incisively. This can give us the strength of irrevocable absolutes in a twenty-first-century society mired in relativism.

A Response to Crisis or Tragedy

The introduction is especially crucial when the sermon is in response to a particular crisis or tragedy in the congregation, community, nation, or world. The situation or concern is already on people's minds. Once again, allow me to illustrate.

One of the most outstanding young men in my Hollywood church was killed in a tragic auto accident. The parents were devastated. Daily they had claimed the promise that God would protect their children. What could people say to the family now?

The following Sunday we could not proceed as if nothing had happened. So the sermon I was going to preach was set aside so I could give pastoral care to the entire congregation. The grief of one family stirred the unhealed grief in many others. And so I began:

> It's on all our minds. So let's talk about it. One of our families has endured a heart-shattering loss. Deep questions have

been stirred in all of us. How could God have allowed this to happen? Why is there suffering?

No less concern must be expressed in community and national crises. I remember the Sunday after the Los Angeles riots in 1992. The sermon had to address the animosity between the black and Filipino communities. As I was working on the introduction to a communion sermon on reconciliation, I received many calls about the turmoil in our city. Two calls stood out. A black member called to unload his growing hatred for the Filipinos who were taking over black businesses in his neighborhood. That call was followed by one from an irate Filipino, whose store had been looted by rioting blacks.

The text I had selected for my message was, "If you bring your gift to the altar, and there remember that your brother has something against you, leave your gift there before the altar, and go your way. First be reconciled to your brother, and then come and offer your gift" (Matthew 5:23-24). The introduction to the communion meditation began like this:

> "I hate 'em! I hate 'em!" These same angry words were shouted over the phone by two men in two different calls, both expressing hostility against each other's race as a result of destruction of each other's rights and property during the riots during this last week. Both men are Christians, both are Presbyterians, both are members of this church, and both are here for communion this morning. I have talked to both of them at length, separately and then together. I told both of them that reconciliation is not an option for a Christian, and if they came to communion without being reconciled, the living Christ would demand that they be reconciled before they came to the communion table to receive the bread and wine. I am happy to say that they have been reconciled. In fact, they have agreed to come forward at the end of this message and serve each other the communion.

What has happened to these men needs to happen to all of us after this turbulent week. Christ stands in front of the table. He invites you to come and receive His grace, but also He cautions you to first be reconciled in your own heart with those from whom you may be estranged, and then come. Let's take seriously Christ's words in the Sermon on the Mount in which He calls for this level of accountability.

This pointed introduction was followed by an exposition of Matthew 5:23-24 and Paul's challenge for us to be agents of reconciliation in 2 Corinthians 5:19 and then by the sacrament and the witness of two men whose bitterness had been healed.

Differing Methods Among Differing Preachers

Some of the best preachers of history differ greatly in how they started their sermons:

- Robert Murray McCheyne's introductions were generally weak, almost nonexistent. He usually began with an exposition of words and phrases of his text and only occasionally did he make a statement of his theme.

- A contemporary of John Henry Newman commented on his preaching: "Three things impress us. First, the directness of the address. He gets to work promptly, drives straight at his mark, and closes with a direct appeal."

- Study of the sermons of Washington Gladden reveals that his introductions were always brief.

- As an admirer of the sermons of G. Campbell Morgan, I was interested to read a firsthand account of his introductions. Alexander Gammie, in *Preachers I Have Heard*, wrote,

"Morgan appeared stiff and awkward at the beginning of the sermon. But once he had plunged into his subject, there was a wonderful transformation. The whole man appeared to palpitate with an uncontrollable energy. he preached with every fiber of his being. He cultivated neither daintiness of style nor sensationalism of speech, neither a wealth of paradox nor a display of phrasecraft. He fed his hearers strong meat..."[17]

- Karl Barth stuck to biblical introductions, believing that the preceding portions of the service served as introductions so that he did not need to do much introducing.

- Dietrich Bonhoeffer did not believe that he should depend heavily on the introduction or a complicated scheme of construction. He believed that the text gave form to the sermon and the sooner into the text, the better. His sermons were composed of the three elements of teaching, edification, and evangelism.

- Helmut Thielicke, on the other hand, gave a great deal of attention to his introductions. He used them to establish immediate contact with his audience and state the theme of his message. He established rapport with the contemporary mind and laid the groundwork for the theme of the message. Penetrating questions that he answered in the body of the sermon often served as the main thrust of the introduction.

My observation from reading sermons of preachers through Christian history has led me to the conclusion that those who gave little attention to their introductions could have been more effective if they had spent more time preparing them. I see that the success of others was measurably increased because of the time spent polishing their preparation of the strategic opening minutes of their sermons.

Humorous Anecdotes

A concluding word about introductions must acknowledge that sometimes a bit of humor to introduce a sermon is effective, especially if it involves an incident that enables the preacher to laugh at himself or herself. Here's one I used from an experience on a busy afternoon in the week before Christmas:

> Ever get stressed out by people blowing their car horns behind you? Well, I did during this past week. It was one of those "It's just a few days before Christmas and I've got to finish up my last minute shopping before it's too late!" kind of afternoons. I had entered a busy mall parking lot, gotten my parking stub from an attendant, been reminded to have it validated, put the stub in my shirt pocket, parked my car, and rushed into a store where I spent more money buying gifts than I would have if I had done my shopping earlier. I carried two large bags of purchases to my car and put them into the trunk. As I attempted to drive out of the parking lot, I was stopped by an attendant at a gate and asked for my validated parking stub.
>
> You guessed it: I had forgotten to have it validated. I appealed to the attendant, "I have made lots of purchases, they are all in the trunk, but here's the cashier's receipt of my purchases."
>
> "Sorry, mister," the grim and demanding attendant said, "You have to have a validated parking stub or I'll have to charge you five dollars."
>
> At that moment a car pulled up behind me at the exit gate. It seemed like about three seconds before the woman in the car began to blow her car horn. She was relentless.
>
> Her horn kept blasting as I wrestled to release my seat

belt and tried to reach into my pants pocket for the five dollars, as the attendant insistently held out her hand, flexing her fingers in a demanding gesture of impatience. All I had in my pocket was a ten-dollar bill. So, all I could do was offer it to the attendant and ask for change. Meanwhile, the woman in the car behind mine kept leaning on her horn.

Now, I think you know that I'm a very level-spirited man, and would like to be known as one with great understanding of the proclivities of human nature. (Smile here with an overindulgent condescension.) Well, I have to tell you that I lost it!

Suddenly, I got out of my car and walked back to the persistent horn blower's car. I asked her to roll down her car door window. In a calm voice that hid my consternation, I said, "Would you do me a favor? Please get out of your car and go sit in the driver's seat of mine and I will get into your driver's seat and blow your horn!" The look on the woman's face slowly shifted from impatient anger, to utter amazement, and finally to a smile she could not withhold. Then she began to laugh. And so did I. We exchanged Christmas greetings and I returned to my car. As I pulled out of the parking lot, I looked into the rearview mirror. The woman was still laughing and waving.

Ever lose the true spirit of Christmas in the preparation for Christmas? Well, I almost did. So this morning I want you to join me as we prepare to make this the best Christmas of our lives. And during the sermon I hope no one in a car in the church parking lot blows his or her horn!

In Summary

Now to summarize what we have discussed about introductions of sermons, allow me to put it in several positive admonitions:

- Vary the types of introductions.

- Write them out with great care.

- Prepare the introduction after your research is completed and the thrust of the sermon is clear in your mind.

Be sure the introduction meets these five tests:

1. Arrests attention.

2. Establishes your empathy.

3. States the biblical text.

4. Clarifies the purpose of the sermon.

5. Affirms what the "take away" will be for the listener.

Memorize the introduction so you can give it looking the congregation in the eye.

May it always be said of you and me what was said of Phillips Brooks after his preparation of the sermon manuscript was completed: "The sermon was now in Brooks himself, like a banked furnace waiting to break forth with heat."[18]

Chapter 8

Thirty Minutes to Raise the Dead

John Ruskin has given us a vivid description of the purpose of a sermon. He said that "preaching is thirty minutes to raise the dead." I agree.

Prior to meeting Christ and committing our lives to Him we are the walking dead—spiritually, intellectually, emotionally, and volitionally. The term *life* is used 36 times in the New Testament as a synonym for our Lord and the Christian life. It is one of the great names given our Lord; it is used by Him to describe who He is and what He came to do; it is a composite term to dramatize what happens to a person who believes in Him; it is the word to explain the miracle of the character and personality transformation that takes place when we abide in Him and He abides in us; and it is a metonym for an endless joy in heaven.

Again, for emphasis, preaching is the communication of life: life as Christ lived it, life as we live it in Him as recipients of the efficacy of His cross and resurrection, and life as He lives it in us as our indwelling Lord.

With this dialogical focus in mind, now let's turn our attention to the actual writing of the body of the sermon. It must carefully be outlined before we write it and commit it to memory. Outlining with main points and subheads is crucial to be sure there is a flow of thought arising out of the biblical text.

For example, under the Roman numeral II, "Body of Thought" (I being "Introduction" and III "Conclusion"), the basic points can be listed alphabetically. As I mentioned, it is good to vary the number of these to avoid predictable sameness and to allow the Holy Spirit to determine the number. Be careful not to coerce the text into the same number of points every week. Clearly stated points really provide great freedom in the delivery of the sermon. We will deal with that in greater detail in the chapter on the presentation of the sermon.

> We should thoroughly explain the primary passage we are expositing. This provides lasting biblical education as well as inspiration for our people.

For me, a verse or passage of the Bible always must be the basis of the sermon. Even topical preaching must be rooted in the authoritative Word of God. Though we draw from other rich biblical passages, historical and contemporary anecdotes, and our own experiences and insight to illustrate the basic verse or paragraph of Scripture on which the sermon is based, we should thoroughly explain the primary passage we are expositing. This provides lasting biblical education as well as inspiration for our people.

Here is an illustration of one of my sermons. I will include the entire message in an effort to show the strong link between the introduction and what follows in the content in the main exposition of a verse or passage of Scripture. (Further illustrations of the body of thought will follow in the next two chapters).

The sermon was entitled "Life's Ultimate Question" and was based on Matthew 16:13-28. It may be helpful as an illustration of the interlocking aspects of the sermon. I am going to share with you the introduction in some detail because I hope it will illustrate the desire to identify with the congregation while quickly getting into the biblical passage and then making the application as clear as possible.

People's destiny, now and forever, is at stake when preaching on such a text. The challenge is to acknowledge the frame of mind and mood in which they arrived in the sanctuary and move them on to life's ultimate question. Drawing them into the exposition gives them a chance to catch their breath before the challenging thrusts of the points of the body of thought.

This message was preached when I was a guest preacher at a prominent church in Washington DC where solid biblical exposition is expected—but also in a city often so consumed by the tyranny of the urgent that life's ultimate question might seem irrelevant. I thought that not asking it would be irreverent!

This was a Sunday morning on which I was clearly guided to focus on people's personal relationship with Christ. So, for whatever it is worth, here is one of my efforts to preach a message with empathy, biblical exposition, application, and a call for commitment.

> Unless I miss my guess, there is a question lurking in the minds of many of you. You might think it would be improper to blurt it out, but you honestly wish you could. What's more, you may wonder if you'd find an answer to your question if you got someone's attention!
>
> You have come to worship with hopes and hurts, fondest unfulfilled dreams and desires, frustrations and fears. You also may feel that your personal needs are insignificant when compared to the national and international crises swirling around you. And yet, your question persists.
>
> Here's what I suspect you really want to know: Will being here this morning make any difference? That may be your most urgent question. But you're not the only one here who has a question this morning.
>
> There is Someone here who is asking life's *ultimate* question. And He is asking it of you! And of me! The Living Christ is here! The startling thing is that *how we answer His question will make all the difference in our lives this morning*. Amazing, isn't it? We come with a question, and the answer is in our response to the most crucial question that we could

ever be asked. What is that question? It sounds in our souls as we hear it in the biblical context in which Christ first asked it. Then we can grapple with its implications to us and the urgency of how we answer it.

Christ first asked life's ultimate question on the road to Caesarea Philippi. Few places could have provided a more significant setting. Jesus, walking ahead of His disciples, was silhouetted against the city in all its Roman glory. Rising up out of its center was a translucent temple of white marble built by Herod the Great in honor of the Caesars. Around it were magnificent villas and palaces added by Herod's son Philip, who had renamed the city to honor Caesar and to impress his own name upon history! The power of Rome was in the air, but so were the hauntingly vivid memories of worship of the pagan god Baal—once so powerful in the region. In fact, before Philip renamed it the city had been called Banias or Panias in honor of the Greek god of the wild, Pan. Ruins of the temples and shrines of Baal orgy worship punctuated the landscape.

Framing the view and overshadowing the region was Mount Hermon, metaphor of Israel's quest for God. Undoubtedly, sharp recollections filled the disciples' minds of the strategic times God had encountered great leaders of Israel on that mountain. On the slope of Hermon, a cliff filled with ancient inscriptions and niches containing statues of pagan gods gave stark reminder of the conflict Israel had faced maintaining its monotheism against syncretism, the blending of religions and their gods.

It was here, in this region of ambiguous symbols of humankind's lust for military might and the religious quest for meaning, that Jesus stopped, turned, and confronted His disciples with a penultimate question: "Who do men say that I am?"

This was not the question of an insecure leader seeking to know his standing in the public opinion polls. It was a probing inquiry designed to determine the extent to which people were discovering His true identity, mission, and message.

The answers were really very complimentary. The disciples rehearsed the speculations they had heard. They told Jesus that the fears of Herod Antipas, who had murdered John the Baptist, had promoted the theory that He was John raised from the dead. Others speculated from the prophecy of Malachi that He might be Elijah come to prepare the way for the Messiah. Still others surmised that the vision given to Judas Maccabaeus was being realized: He was Jeremiah, who had come with a golden sword to wage war for the deliverance of Israel. And some simply said Jesus was one of the prophets.

It was at this significant moment following what others said about Him that Jesus pressed home His *ultimate* question. Surrounded by geographical and topographical evidences of humankind's longing for an answer to the riddle of life, and in the context of the varied but false opinions about His real identity, Jesus asked the ultimate question: "But who do you say that I am?"

Only one could find his voice to answer. Simon's response was seasoned by deep thought and motivated by a gift of faith from the Father. His face was radiant and his voice alive with the excitement and insight as he answered, "You are the Christ." (Matthew's Gospel records the full statement: "You are the Christ, the Son of the living God"—Matthew 16:16.)

Clearly Simon acknowledged Jesus not as forerunner of the Messianic age, but as the Messiah Himself. This had been hinted at before early in the Master's ministry when Andrew and John had announced to Simon that they had found the Messiah. When Simon first met the Master, He had said to him, "You are Simon the son of Jonah. You shall be called Cephas (which is translated, A Stone)." John 1:42. Now, as a fact of revelation from the Spirit of the Father, in this moment of high spiritual drama, Simon knew for himself that it was true: Jesus was the expected Messiah! And he knew too that this beloved and winsome Person with the dust of Palestine on His sandals and the salvation of the world in His heart was the Son of God.

We too are surrounded by the different ways many people have tried to answer the question about who Christ is. Today people would be quick to offer answers: He is a historical character…a poetic idealist…a sensitive, but misguided person who is obsolete in our cybernetic, techno-political world…a fine ethical and moral teacher and example…the greatest human being who ever lived. Even among traditional Christians there is some equivocation about who Christ is to us today. Among liberal theologians, the divinity of Christ has been an open question in theological discussions. And in many circles of both clergy and laity a kind of faithless familiarity keeps people from being forthright in answering life's ultimate question.

Also today, when we are so afraid of offending people of other religions, there is an equation that dominates much of our culture: *inclusiveness multiplied by relativism equals exclusion*. Allow me to explain. In our efforts to be sure we are accepting and affirming of other religions, we tend to end up very vague about our own beliefs. Relativism, which asserts that everything is relative and that there are no absolutes, has had a debilitating impact on our culture, churches, and many Christians.

I like the statement of a rabbi friend: "You be who you are so I can be who I am!" And I will not soon forget the concern of a Muslim who said, "Don't deny your own beliefs in an effort to be so solicitously accepting of mine that you become unsure of what you believe, because then I'll never know what a real Christian is!" What he was saying was, "Don't include me out!"

In the midst of all the vacillating voices answering Christ's question "Who do men say that I am?" He comes to each of us and puts the penetratingly personal question, "But who do you, for yourself, say that I am?" Christ is not even satisfied with how we might have answered years ago— He is most concerned about who He is to us now. This morning. Right now. How will you answer? Your answer is tremendously important!

Our answer is dependent on our convictions about the authenticity of the biblical account of the life, message, death, and resurrection of Christ. Do you believe that He is who he said He was? He claimed to be the Messiah, the incarnate Son of God, Immanuel, God with us, our Savior and Lord. Robert Browning presses the point: "What think ye of Christ, friend, when all's done and said. Like you this Christianity or not?"[19]

The biblical Jesus is not the Jesus we have created of our own making and faking—an easygoing, good-natured Jesus who is on call when we want Him to help us deal with our own personal agendas. Having only this culturalized, benevolent, but somewhat weak "errand-boy" Jesus stunts our spiritual growth. "It's a sniveling modern invention," said George Bernard Shaw, "for which there is no warrant in the Gospels."[20] And C.S. Lewis focused the issue sharply:

A man who was merely a man and said the sort of things Jesus said wouldn't be a great moral teacher. He'd either be a

> lunatic—on the level of a man who says he is a poached egg—
> or else he'd be the devil of hell. You must make your choice.
> Either this man was, and is the son of God, or else a madman or
> something worse. Christianity, if false, is of no importance, and
> if true, of infinite importance. The one thing it cannot be is mod-
> erately important.[21]

The robust, challenging Jesus also confronts us, and He will not accept second place in our lives. He calls us to the exhilarating adventure of dynamic discipleship. Though He meets us as we are with incredible grace, He loves us too much to leave us as we've been. The authentic Jesus of the Bible tenderly cares for us when we hurt, but He tenaciously exposes anything that keeps us from being all He intends for us to be. His love and forgiveness are unqualified, but also His demands are unequivocal. He is the Master who holds before us the mandate of the kingdom of God, and the Lord of all life who calls us to commit all we have and are to Him.

This true Jesus spoke what have been called "hard say-ings," hard not because they are difficult to understand, but that they are difficult to live. His ultimate question perhaps is the hardest of all if we want to be absolutely honest in how we answer. "Who am I to you, really?" That cuts like a laser into the core of our being and forces us to evaluate whether our priorities, values, and attitudes match a forthright dec-laration that—for us—Christ is indeed our Lord and Savior.

How we answer Christ's ultimate question determines what we will receive from Him this morning for the five most urgent needs of our lives.

First, our answer will determine how much we know and experience of God our Father and the Holy Spirit, our source of supernatural power.

Jesus clearly declared that He came from the pre-existent Father and the Holy Spirit. He asserted that He was the condescension of divinity and the exaltation of the intended potential of humankind. No feckless guru could pull off a claim like that! Note His own words, "I proceeded forth and came from God; nor have I come of Myself, but He sent me" (John 8:42). Awesome.

From before creation and measured time, He was a Person in the pre-existent glory circle of the Trinity—Father, Son, and Holy Spirit. He came from His position in this circle of mutual glorification to reveal the Father and promise the outpouring of the Holy Spirit. He continues as reigning Lord and comes to each of us to invite us into that glory circle to know the unqualified love and forgiveness of the Father and the empowering of the Holy Spirit. At one time He is the portrait of the Father and the prototype of what humankind was meant to be and can be, in and through Him.

Christ could not have been clearer than He was in His declaration: "I am the way, the truth, and the life. No one comes to the Father except through Me" (John 14:6). It is equally true that the Father continues to come to us in Christ and through the Holy Spirit constantly seeks to give us the gift of faith to entrust our lives to Christ. We cannot bypass Christ to get to God, for God has willed it otherwise. We must come to grips with His message, accept His death as atonement for our sins, believe that He is alive, and dare to live under His lordship.

Second, how we answer Christ's ultimate question determines our ability to live the abundant life He promised. "I have come that you might have life and have it abundantly" (John 10:10, author's paraphrase). "Lo, I am with you always"

(Matthew 28:20). He sustains us in loneliness and gives us strength in our weaknesses. He gives us guidance in indecision and wisdom in confusion. "Abide in Me, and I in you" (John 15:4). If we can answer Christ's ultimate question with bold conviction and then invite Him to make us His post-resurrection home, the mysterious miracle of a character transplant begins and continues every day of our lives.

That's what Christ promised Simon, the big fisherman, that day at Caesarea Philippi when he answered His ultimate question. In Matthew's account it reads, "Blessed are you, Simon Bar-Jonah, for flesh and blood has not revealed this to you, but My Father who is in heaven. And I also say to you that you are Peter, and on this rock I will build My church, and the gates of Hades shall not prevail against it" (Matthew 16:17-18).

The disciple was promised a new name that implied a total change of character. No longer vacillating Simon, the son of Jonah, but now a rocklike person, Peter—*petros* in Greek, meaning "rock." In the Greek text, Simon is called *Petros,* but it is upon "this rock," *petra*, meaning a mass of rock, that the church will be built. I think this *petra* is our faith. The church was never to be built on a human personality, but on the rock of faith. When we answer Jesus' ultimate question, claiming Him as our Lord and Savior, He gives us a new name and unshakable, massive rocklike faith and uses us to build up His church.

Third, how we answer Christ's ultimate question determines our ability to receive and give forgiveness. As tools for living the abundant life, Christ offers us the keys of the kingdom: "I will give you the keys of the kingdom of heaven, and whatever you bind on earth will be bound in heaven, and whatever you loose on earth will be loosed in heaven" (Matthew

16:19). We are given the power to loose or bind people. The authority of absolution is given to everyone who believes in Christ. We can free people with forgiveness or bind them with a refusal to forgive.

This is true in our relationships. Forgiveness was so important to Christ that the phrase in the Lord's Prayer about forgiving our debtors as we have been forgiven our debts was the only one He felt it necessary to stress and explain with urgency: "If you forgive men their trespasses, your heavenly Father will also forgive you. But if you do not forgive men their trespasses, neither will your Father forgive your trespasses" (Matthew 6:14-15).

What a demanding challenge! We can hold people at the arm's length of judgmentalism, or set them free with forgiveness. The Greek word for forgiveness is *aphesis,* the noun form of the verb *aphiemi,* a compound word combining *apo,* "from," and *hiemi,* "to send." Forgiveness sends away the hurts, the slights and oversights, the anguish and pain of remembered failure—our own and others'.

We are reminded of Isaiah's prophecy of the power of Christ as our scapegoat. Drawing on the image of the practice of the scapegoat in Leviticus 16:22, Isaiah wrote, "Surely He has borne our griefs and carried our sorrows" (Isaiah 53:4). The Hebrew word for "borne" is *nasa,* "to lift up, carry away, remove to a distance away," and the word for "carried," *sabal,* means an actual substitution. The sins of the people were pinned onto a goat and it was led out into the wilderness to die. People's sins were carried away and totally removed. Christ, our scapegoat, has taken our sins and carried them away. He continues to do that each time we turn over to Him our unforgiven memories. .

Here is the double negative that equals the gospel's

great positive: grace is receiving the forgiveness we do not deserve and His mercy is not receiving the punishment we do deserve! And you and I are given the same grace and mercy to share with others. The Lord has given us the power to send away the hurt or harm people have done to us, themselves, and others. Even when we think they don't deserve forgiveness or have never even confessed the need of it from us, we are commanded to forgive. The twist of reality is that if we don't, we too are bound with the hurting memory. As one woman said, "I love myself as loved by Christ too much to not forgive."

This quality of Christly grace is motivated by the fourth result of our answer to Christ's ultimate question. When we answer, committing our lives to him, we are ready to receive the mysterious but transforming dynamic of the dual cross—Christ's cross and our own.

Fourth, how we answer Christ's ultimate question, committing our lives to Him, determines our experience of the death-and-resurrection cycle we are called to share with Christ.

That day at Caesarea Philippi, after Peter's confession, Christ's declaration of how He would build His church on those who receive the gift of faith, and the awesome entrusting of the power of absolution, He immediately pressed on to tell His disciples that He must go on to Jerusalem. There He would suffer and be killed, but on the third day would rise from the dead.

This so shocked Peter that He rebuked the Master and said, "Far be it from You, Lord; this shall never happen to you!" (Matthew 16:22). The disciple's new gift of faith did not reach to trusting the Lord to this excruciating extent. His protest brought a bracing rebuke from Jesus: "Get behind Me, Satan! You are an offense to Me, for you are not mindful of the things of God, but the things of men" (Matthew 16:23).

Satan? But this was Simon Bar-Jonah! How could he be called "Satan"? Jesus knew that Simon didn't simply react out of misguided loyalty or distorted ambition, but that Satan, the dissembler, distresser, and dissuader of people from seeking and doing the will of God had found a viable pawn in volatile, vacillating Simon. Jesus also knew that the most vulnerable time in the life of a new believer in Him would be shortly after verbal confession of his or her life. Our greatest temptations come not only in times of discouragement and depression, but following our initial or successive steps in living out our faith.

That's when we need to experience the transforming dynamic of the dual cross: the mysterious but open secret of victorious living, the dual cross to face the double crosses of life. "If anyone desires to come after Me," Christ told His disciples, "let him deny himself, take up his cross, and follow Me" (Matthew 16:24; Mark 8:34). Christ's cross was the once-never-to-be-repeated substitutionary sacrifice for the sins of the world. Our cross, however, means our death to self and a resurrection to a totally new life. It also means our surrender of our wills to faithful obedience to seeking and following the guidance of Christ.

We trivialize the cross's true meaning when we say of some situation, difficult person, or physical or psychological problem, "Well, that's my cross!" Not so! The death and resurrection cycle of Christ is recapitulated in us, over and over again. That is why the apostle Paul said, "I die daily" (1 Corinthians 15:31). But he also said, "...that I may know Him and the power of His resurrection, and the fellowship of His sufferings [*pathematon*], being conformed to his death, if

by any means, I may attain to the resurrection of the dead...
One thing I do, forgetting those things which are behind
and reaching forward to those things which are ahead, I
press toward the goal for the prize of the upward call of God
in Christ Jesus" (Philippians 3:10-11). Those who take up
their cross in unreserved surrender of self, and death to their
own control of everything and everyone, are given the life-
changing gift of the indwelling Christ.

"Christ in you, the hope of glory" (Colossians 1:27) was
the apostle Paul's way of explaining it. His control of his old
self had died in his commitment to Christ and now was
the riverbed for the flow of Christ's Spirit through him. He
wrote about this secret of character transformation to the
Galatians: "I have been crucified with Christ; it is no longer
I who live, but Christ lives in me; and the life which I now
live in the flesh I live by faith in the Son of God, who loved
me and gave Himself for me" (Galatians 2:20).

We were never meant to be a river of self-generated
insight, strength, and adequacy; we were meant to be the
riverbed for the flow of the character of Christ through our
personalities. The fruit of the Spirit is really a description
of what we are to expect and express when this magnificent character transplant remakes us in the image of Christ:
love, *joy,* peace, longsuffering, kindness, goodness, faithfulness, gentleness, self-control (Galatians 5:22).

Our relationships are radically altered as we live in fellowship with Christ and are the riverbed for the flow of His
Spirit. The depth of His love heals us and makes us unselfish
lovers of people. Joy, so much greater than mere happiness,
radiates from us. A profound peace of mind controls our
thinking and makes us peacemakers. The Lord's patience
gives us calmness in our struggles. We are amazed at the

consistent surge of kindness we feel that makes us affirmers of people. And this newfound character strength has the consistency of Christ's goodness. Just as the Lord's faithfulness never ends, we develop a dependability and indefatigable strength never to give up on other people or frustrating situations. The meekness we experience is not weakness, but the result of living life under the control of the Master. Remarkably, we have greater self-control! than we ever thought possible. Christ gives us the strength to fulfill John's challenge, "Anyone who says he is a Christian should live as Christ did" (1 John 2:6 TLB). That happens when we *admit* our need for Christ, *submit* our lives to Christ, *remit* our control to Christ, and *transmit* our love for Christ to others.

Henry Drummond said, "To become Christlike is the only thing in the world worth caring for, the thing before which every ambition is folly and lower achievements vain."[22]

A person who experienced this character transplant said, "I was a sour note on Adam's reed when the Master musician reorchestrated my life and gave the angels something to sing about!" Indeed, through Him we are more than we ever thought we could be! But not just for this portion of our lives on earth, but for the time of our physical death and then forever.

And that brings us to our fifth and concluding point: *How we answer Christ's ultimate question determines our courage to face death and where we will spend eternity.* Underneath all anxieties is the fear of dying. Not so for us, if we belong to Christ. On the night before He was crucified, He prayed, "This is eternal life, that they may know You, the only true God, and Jesus Christ whom You have sent" (John 17:3). He went to the cross to defeat the forces of evil and death. He rose from the dead. Death was swallowed up in victory. His promise was fulfilled: "I am the resurrection and the life. He who believes in me, though he may die, he shall live. And whoever lives and believes in Me shall never die" (John 11:25-26). Christ followed this liberating promise with another piercing question, "Do you believe this?" Well, do you? Do I? If He truly is Christ to us, death has lost its sting. All because we are sure where we will spend eternity. We will all live forever. But are you completely confident of where? With Whom?

John the apostle was very clear: "He who has the Son has life; he who has not the Son has not life" (1 John 5:12). A person may go to heaven without health, riches, honor, learning, or friends, but he can never go there without Christ!

When we commit our lives to Christ in response to His ultimate question, we are ushered into eternal life now. This makes our physical death only a transition in living forever. Spiritual death to self comes in a complete surrender of our lives to Christ. This *is* a primary conviction of biblical Christianity. Paul explained the wonder of this assurance in Romans 6:8-11:

> If we died with Christ, we believe that we shall also live with Him, knowing that Christ, having been raised from the dead, dies no more. Death no longer has dominion over Him. For the death that He died, He died to sin once for all; but the life that He lives, He lives to God. Likewise, you also reckon yourselves to be dead to sin, but alive to God in Christ Jesus our Lord.

At the point of our physical demise, it will be said,

> Grief for you would surely be wrong,
> You took life on tiptoe, firm and strong.

Death came no conjurer in the end;
You simply rose to meet Christ, your Friend.

And we will know Him because of the profound friendship we have shared with Him all through this initial phase of eternity. He will have been with us through all the trials of life, turning our struggles into stepping-stones. And then at the point of physical cessation, He will embrace us and walk with us through the valley of the shadow of death and into heaven.

Are you sure of that for you?

The living Christ is here! And now, in this quiet moment, He moves from person to person, taking each of us by the shoulders and looking into our eyes as He whispers into our souls, "Who do *you* say that I am? Really! Who am I for you personally? Am I truly your Lord and Savior? Will you accept My unqualified love and forgiveness for you? Do you invite Me to live in you? Will you commit yourself to be My disciple? Do you want Me to set you free to love others as I have loved you? Do you want My strength for your responsibilities at home, in government, in society, and in your nation? Will you accept My wisdom for your decisions, My courage to live as My disciple, My will for your future, My power to live without anxiety and fear? Would you like to be free of any worry about death, and be absolutely sure that you will live forever?"

Everything, now and for eternity, depends on your answer.

As part of our discussion of preaching with passion, I appreciate your reading through this sermon. My hope is that it will illustrate my effort to use the preparation time to develop a unity of the introduction, body, and completion of a sermon. In a subsequent chapter, we will consider preaching about the cross to "underwhelmed" church people.

Now, allow me a personal word: at the conclusion of the worship service in which the above sermon was preached, I greeted the congregation in the narthex of the church building. I was deeply moved and all the more committed to preaching when a senator came up to me and exclaimed, "It happened. After you finished your sermon, Christ did come to me as you told us He would. I said 'Yes!' to all His questions!"

As I shared the man's sheer joy, I was assured again that the essence of preaching with passion is to bring men and women face-to-face with Jesus Christ and to answer life's ultimate question.

Now, let's press on with further discussion and illustrations of the development of the sermon.

Chapter 9

Communicating God-Esteem

Having reviewed an entire sermon in the previous chapter, now I want to share some additional examples of the body-of-thought section of sermons. I have selected some that communicate God-esteem, that magnificent assurance of being chosen, called, and cherished by God that gives a person a sense of being valued and given a destiny. It far surpasses self-esteem based only on self-confidence. God-inspired esteem leads to praise; self-esteem to pride.

I am persuaded that the task of the preacher is not to remind people how bad they are, but to proclaim how great God is! Our privilege is to help them see themselves through the gracious eyes of God. This positive approach not only helps them receive His power to change, but also to take the crucial steps of growth.

To illustrate that, consider a sermon on Psalm 8:4-5:

> What is man that You are mindful of him,
> And the son of man that You visit him?
> For you have made him a little lower than the angels,
> And You have crowned him with glory and honor.

An exposition of the text reveals that the word for *angels* in Hebrew is *elohim*, a name for God. The verse may be translated, "You have made him a little lower than God" (NASB), or by implication, "a little lower than Yourself." This approach is confirmed by what follows: "…And You have crowned him with glory and honor." These are attributes of

God Himself. He came in Jesus Christ to reveal who He is and what we were meant to be when we are transformed and filled with His Spirit.

Transitioning to the Body of Thought

A sermon on a topic such as "Living at Full Potential" based on Psalm 8 may be introduced with a statement something like this:

> I invite you to join me in a grand experiment. Imagine you have God's vision and heart. Now I want you to see yourself from His perspective and vision for your life. Looking at yourself and your realm of your responsibility, what do you see? Two things will determine what you see: your conception of God and your own attitude toward your life. If your understanding of God is limited to a cosmic judge who is full of wrath for your failures and mistakes, what you will see of yourself through the eyes of that kind of god will be confining and oppressive. If, however, your image of God is that He forgives even before you ask, He loves you unreservedly, He wants the very best for your life, and He has given you a realm of responsibility in which He will crown you with His honor and glory, then you will see yourself through His eyes and will be filled with authentic God-inspired esteem, zest, and excitement for living. Psalm 8 is a clarion call to live at full potential in the realm of responsibility entrusted to us. This leads us to the steps necessary for living out the glory and honor the Lord has bestowed on us.

The outline of the body of thought follows naturally:

II. Body of Thought

    A. Crowned for your realm

    B. Claim your realm

C. Consecrate your realm

D. Commit yourself to excellence in your realm

E. Count on supernatural power to serve in your realm

A sermon on how God is at work to strengthen us in our weaknesses may be based on Romans 8:26-28. Especially underline verse 28:

> Likewise the Spirit also helps us in our weaknesses. For we do not know what we should pray for as we ought, but the Spirit Himself makes intercession for us with groanings which cannot be uttered. And He Who searches the hearts knows what the mind of the Spirit is, because He makes intercession for the saints according to the will of God. And we know that all things work together for good to those who love God, to those who are the called according to His purpose.

Careful exposition of this text will reveal that in the early Greek manuscripts, God is the subject of the twenty-eighth verse: *ho Theos*, God, is the subject of *sunergei*, works together. It should be rendered, "And we know that *God works all things together* for good to those who love God, to those who are the called according to His purpose."

As part of a transition to the body of thought in the light of this exposition, I like to tell an account of a liberating experience in the life of Senator Max Cleland from Georgia at a Bible study in the Senate.

> Max lost both of his legs just above the knees and his right hand in the Vietnam War. It happened when, as a platoon leader, he led his men off a helicopter and down a path toward combat. Suddenly he saw a grenade rolling between his legs. He leaped on it to save his men. It exploded and maimed him for life. All through the subsequent years of his life, he has lived with the horrifying, guilt-producing

thought that it had been his grenade. A heart-thumping dream recaptured this excruciating event most every night.

One day Max was rolled into the senators' weekly Bible study in his wheelchair. His face was ashen white. He looked tired and distressed.

"Max, are you alright?" Senator Trent Lott asked. "No, not really," Max replied in a stressed voice. Then he told the senators at the Bible study about his recurring dream and the memory that prompted it. The senators listened intently and then suggested we wait to begin the Bible study and pray for healing of Max's memory. The senators' prayers were very moving as they asked the Lord to strengthen Max to endure and to liberate him from this debilitating memory.

Max remained for the Bible study on Romans 8:26-28. The emphasis was on the correct translation of 8:28. We developed a motto: "Things don't work out; God works out things." Max claimed that the next day when he did an interview for the History Channel about his experience of losing his legs and right arm, he reiterated the account the way he had told it to the other senators the day before.

When the program aired a few days later, a man by the name of David Lloyd in Annapolis was watching. It brought back memories for him too. He had been the medical officer in Max's platoon that day in Vietnam. As the program ended, he knew he had to call the senator. When he reached him he said, "Max, your memory of that day in Vietnam is all wrong. I was the medic on duty with you and wrapped up your leg stubs. That was not your grenade! A raw recruit who leaped out of the helicopter behind you had loosened the pins in the grenades in his grenade belt. One popped out and rolled down under your feet. You leaped on it to save your men. I know; I was there!"

Max recounts that learning this liberating news was like another explosion, but this one was in his mind. He no longer needed to blame himself for the accident. He received the gift of God-esteem.

A four-point body of thought follows that introduction:

1. Things don't work out; God works out things: exposition of the text.

2. How God strengthens us in our weakness. J.B. Phillips: "Helps us in our present limitations."

3. God is on time, in time, for our time of need.

4. What are the things you need to surrender to God for Him to work them together for good: His glory and your growth?

"Losing Heart": A Body-of-Thought Example from Ephesians 3

Last year, as I was preparing a message on Paul's prayer for the Ephesians in Ephesians 3:14-20, I did a contextual analysis of all of Ephesians chapter 3. When I got to verse 13, I came upon a Greek word I had not thought about very much. Actually, the word helped me understand the motivation of Paul's prayer. The apostle's prayer was prayed for Christians who were being tempted to lose heart. They were deeply concerned about the tribulations he was going through in Rome and for the challenges all of the followers of Christ were facing.

It was not easy to be a Christian in Ephesus. Note the verse that immediately precedes the opening of Paul's prayer for them: "I ask that you do not lose heart at my tribulations for you, which is your glory" (verse 13). And then the apostle goes on to tell the Ephesians what he prayed for as antidotes to losing heart. The Greek word for loss of heart

Paul used is *ekkakein*, from the verb *ekkakeo*, to grow weary, lack courage, faint, or lose verve and vitality.

But there is a deeper meaning to *ekkakein*. It also can mean to behave badly and give in to the forces of evil. It can happen when the evidence of evil in the world around us actually draws us into giving in to evil in our own choices or behavior. In Galatians 6:9 Paul uses *ekkakomen*: "Let us not keep giving in to evil while doing good" (author's translation). In 2 Thessalonians 3:13 he uses *ekkakesete*: "Do not grow weary in doing good." In whatever tense, *ekkakein* is a growing hopelessness that brings us to helplessness in temptation. It is a low-grade spiritual fever that is expressed in "Whatever I do, it won't make any difference."

Paul's friends at Ephesus were tempted to discouragement about their own challenges because of what they heard was happening to him in prison. "If this could happen to the great apostle, what chance do we have?" seems to have been their mood.

This background prepared me to write and deliver a sermon on losing heart. After I did an explanation of the meaning of this spiritual malady in the first and twenty-first centuries, I went on to do an exposition of Paul's prayer that follows verse 13 in verses 14-20. I divided the body of thought into the three antidotes to losing heart that he prayed for in what I consider to be one of the most stirring and inspiring passages in the epistles of the New Testament.

Paul's three antidotes:

1. *The supernatural strength of Christ's indwelling spirit*: "to be strengthened with might through His Spirit in the inner man, that Christ may dwell in your hearts by faith" (Ephesians 3:17). The strength of Christ's indwelling Spirit is the first secret of not losing heart. We all need strength for our own set of circumstances in a time when others around us are buckling under and losing heart. Strength is Christ in our inner being: mind, emotions, and will. Inner man: personal,

rational self, the moral I, the essence of a person. Christ may dwell: (*katoikesai*) permanent residence.

2. *Superlative love*: "that you, being rooted and grounded in love, may be able to comprehend [*katalabesthai* from *katalambano*: to grasp, lay hold of with the mind] with all the saints what is the width and length and depth and height— to know [i: to know through experience] the love of Christ which passes [*huperballousan* from *huperballo*—to throw beyond] knowledge [*gnoseos* from verb *ginosko*—to understand completely, to know, to recognize]; that you may be filled with all the fullness of God."

The first dimension of this superlative love is width (*plato*). This means it is initiative and inclusive. Regardless of what we have been, we are called and cherished, set apart to belong first and foremost to the Lord. Nothing can change this. We are His disciples in the rough and tumble of contemporary life. Christ's arms are outstretched and He holds us with the tenderness and strength of His nail-pierced hands. This inclusive love overcomes our self-condemning, self-justifying attitudes. Christ is here reaching out to you who admit how much you need Him, embracing you with the wideness of His mercy. Don't ever forget that grace is receiving love we don't deserve and mercy is not receiving what we do deserve.

But Christ's love is not only wide, but also long (*mekos*). This means that His love is inescapable. There is no place where the Lord is not waiting for us. There is no distance we can go where He is unable to reach us. His embracing arms are long enough to reach us wherever we may have wandered.

Christ's love is also deep (*bathos*). No abyss has ever been found deeper than His love can't sound. When we nurse a memory of failure, or of a relationship we find it difficult to mend, when we ache inside over what people have done to themselves or others, or to us, we rediscover that we cannot ever sink beyond where He can reach us.

But Paul is not finished. He says that Christ's love reaches not only to the depths but also to the heights (*hupsos*)—to the person He has meant us to be, to the unlimited possibilities of the future, to the solution to seemingly unsolvable problems, and at the end of this portion of eternal life, to heaven.

And then to top off all the magnificent promises to those who belong to God through faith in Christ, the apostle goes on to pray for the third antidote to losing heart.

3. *Supreme power*: "To Him who is able to do exceedingly abundantly above all that we ask or think, according to the power that works in us, to Him be glory in the church by Christ Jesus to all generations, forever and ever. Amen" (Ephesians 3:20-21). This is one of the greatest of the "He is able" statements in the epistles. The word "able" is *dunamenoi* from *dunamis*, power. The compound word for "exceedingly abundantly," *hupereksu*, represents Paul's desire to assure the Ephesians, and now us, that we belong to an all-powerful God who will go beyond anything we can imagine to give us an antidote to losing heart. But note: His power works in us to give us the capacity to envision what He is willing and able to do to help, encourage, and inspire us. We need to spend more time seeking His guidance for what to pray than we do making our self-generated petitions. If you have lost heart in any area or relationship of your life, God will give you the power to sense His will and pray for what He has guided you to pray.

Don't miss that it is Christ Jesus, who is the Glorifier,

who is the agent of power to accomplish what will glorify the Father! So, don't lose heart!

I have found that this prayer for the Ephesians became a great source of these antidotes in my life when I prayed through it as it is in Scripture; I then changed the pronouns to be first person, *I* and *me*, as I read it again, experiencing the transforming power available to me; finally I prayed the prayer for my congregation each Sunday morning in the early hours of my own personal devotions.

I did this on my knees. And it was always moving for me to remember that the apostle Paul's expression, "for this reason I bow my knees," probably meant that with his heritage as a Pharisee, he prostrated himself with his face to the floor of his prison room. And don't forget, he was chained to a guard, so the guard would have to have gone down with him and listened to the apostle's prayer. No wonder it was said that they had to rotate the guards away from him because so many were converted to Christ! Why not expect the same for people who are riveted to a passionate preacher?

F.B. Meyer also put it clearly. Expository preaching is "the consecutive treatment of some book or extended portion of Scripture on which the preacher has concentrated head and heart, brain and brawn, over which he has thought and wept and prayed, until it has yielded up its inner secret, and the spirit of it has passed into his spirit."[23] And I would add, can then be passed on to listeners with passion.

While writing our sermons demands rigorous hard work, we will find that these hours often are times when we feel the palpable power of the Spirit give wings to our writing. We will be saved from one preacher's plight:

> His sermon had the usual heads
> And subdivisions fine;
> The language was delicate

And graceful as a vine.
It had its proper opening;
'Twas polished as a whole;
It had but one supreme defect—
It failed to reach the soul.

"The Sainthood of All Believers": An Illustration of the Linkage Between Parts of the Sermon

A further way to communicate God-esteem is to help our congregations claim the true biblical word for a believer. The word is *saint*. Again, allow me to share the entire message to illustrate the close linkage between the introduction, body of thought, and closing. The sermon was entitled "The Sainthood of All Believers."

I. Introduction

Recently, I addressed a presbytery meeting in the Southeast made up of pastors and elders from Presbyterian churches in the area. I began my message by saying, "Good evening, saints!"

My greeting was received with uneasy titters and surprised glances. One man in the audience shouted, "They haven't arrived yet!"

But they had. Every pastor and elder there had confessed Christ as Savior, had received a call into leadership, and to varying degrees was in the awesome process of sanctification. The reaction, however, exemplified how few Christians feel comfortable being called by the New Testament term for believers.

For some, the word *saint* is a term of endearment. The other evening while having dinner in a restaurant, I couldn't help overhearing the conversation of a couple seated nearby. The woman reached across the table and took her husband's hand and said, "Oh, what a saint you are for giving me this evening out!" The man may have been a saint in the true sense, but taking his wife out for dinner did not make him so!

Others use the term *saint* to identify superlative character. "Now there's a real saint," we say when we want to recognize superior spirituality. We imply that not every Christian *is* a saint.

Overheard in Hollywood was this deprecatory statement: "A star you are; a saint you ain't." We wonder what made the person a star, but we also question what behavior kept the person from measuring up to the cultural use of the term *saint*.

We usually think of saints as characters portrayed in stained-glass windows or as heroes or heroines described on the pages of history. In Ambrose Bierce's *The Devil's Dictionary*, a saint is defined as "a dead sinner, revised and edited."

Any desire to claim our biblical rebirth right as saints is further dulled by the practice of canonizing deceased Christians to "sainthood." The Vatican has a special committee responsible for scrutinizing candidates from years gone by. According to my understanding of these qualifications for sainthood, a potential saint must have had a vision of Christ, performed at least two miracles, exemplified superior piety, and mediated healings after his or her death. All the evidence from a person's lifetime and all contemporary claims of miracles are carefully researched and authenticated by this committee.

You might think I am coattailing it when I tell you that a few years ago Rome elevated an Ogilvie to sainthood. He's

Saint John Ogilvie, the last of the Scottish martyrs, martyred in Glasgow in 1611 but distinguished for the healing of cancer patients in recent years.

When I was in Scotland recently, a man in the Highlands remarked, with Calvinist tongue-in-cheek reserve, "Ach, I see one of yer clan made it to sainthood."

A friend who overheard the comment said, "And so have you, Lloyd. You'll never be more or less of a saint than you are right now."

My purpose is not to enter into a polemic about the practice of elevating historic persons to sainthood or about praying in their names, but simply to underline the confusion caused in so many people's minds about their own status as saints today. Protestants generally think of saints as super-Christians. Roman Catholics consider them to be those in heaven who were used mightily on earth.

The term *saint* is used 62 times in the Bible as a synonym for believers. Nowhere is sainthood associated with status earned by performance. The apostle Paul uses the term for believers in Christ in the salutation of his epistles, but always goes on to both affirm and challenge them to press on in sanctification, the essential vocation of sainthood. The first two verses of Ephesians provide us with four dynamics of authentic sainthood, which help us define the kind of saints the local congregation is called to deploy in the world:

> Paul, an apostle of Jesus Christ *by the will of God* to the *saints* who are in Ephesus and *faithful* in Jesus Christ: *Grace* and *peace* from God our Father and the Lord Jesus Christ.

II. Body of Thought

A. Saints are chosen and choose to be chosen

Paul declares that he was an apostle of Jesus Christ by the *will* of God. Here the word *will* comes from the Greek word *thelema* rather than *boulema*. This sets the thematic ambience of the entire epistle. *Thelema* means the desire of God which, to be fully appropriated, requires the cooperation of the human will and spirit. *Boulema* is the immutable, irrevocable will of God. It will be accomplished whether we cooperate or not.

God exercised His *boulema* will when He came in Jesus Christ to reconcile the world to Himself: "God was in Christ reconciling the world" (2 Corinthians 5:19). The verse describes the center of the center of Christianity. God couldn't be stopped. Our sovereign God acted to accomplish His benevolent purpose out of sheer grace. In Jesus Christ, the God-man in the glorious hypostatic union, God revealed who He is and who we were meant to be. Jesus' primary message was the kingdom of God: His rule and reign in us, between us and others, and in all of life. The Messiah went to the cross by the irrevocable will of God. Note that a form of *boulema* is translated as *counsel* in Acts 2:23: "…Him, being delivered up by the determined counsel and foreknowledge of God." No human effort could have stopped the cross.

On Calvary the atoning heart of the Father was revealed and fulfilled. Christ died for us in a once-never-to-be-repeated atonement for our sins and to make us right with God. God exonerated us. He set us free of guilt and condemnation.

By this same immutable will, God, whose Father-heart pulsated in indefatigable love on the cross, raised Christ from the dead. By that same immutability, Christ reigns as

Lord of lords, King of kings, Emmanuel, Savior, Friend. We are recipients of His atonement and are invited into a personal relationship with Him. Christ takes up residence in us as indwelling Lord. We become His postresurrection home! We have been destined to be re-formed in His image.

But not without our willingness. This is where the *thelema* will of God enters in.

Paul became an apostle by the *thelema* will of God. He was elected, called, set apart, and chosen by the desire of God. Yet Paul was not a puppet on a string. He could have resisted his call, but through an encounter with the living Christ, and the gift of faith by the Holy Spirit, Paul was given the power to choose to be chosen.

What does this mean for our sainthood? Everything! By the irrevocable will of God our salvation has been accomplished; by the *thelema* will of God, by His gracious choice, we have been called to receive this salvation.

The first thing we claim in our exposition of sainthood is that we are saints by God's *thelema* will just as surely as Paul was an apostle. When he addressed the saints in Ephesus, he was writing to God's people who stood equally with him as those chosen, called, and cherished.

Paul affirms this in this magnificent first chapter of Ephesians in verses 3-9:

> Blessed be the God and Father of our Lord Jesus Christ, who has blessed us with every spiritual blessing in the heavenly places in Christ, just as He chose us in Him before the foundation of the world, that we should be holy and without blame before Him in love, having *predestined us to adoption* as sons [and daughters!] by Jesus Christ to Himself, according to the good pleasure of His will [note: *thelematos* in the Greek] to the praise of the glory of His grace, by which He made us accepted in the Beloved. In Him

we have redemption through His blood, the forgiveness of sins, according to the riches of His grace which He made to abound toward us in all wisdom and prudence, having made known to us the mystery of His will [*thelematos* again], according to his good pleasure [*eudoxian*], which He purposed in Himself.

B. Saints are holy

But what are we chosen to do? We are chosen to be holy. This is what the word *saint* means. In Greek, the word is *hagios, meaning "set apart, and belonging to God."* It does not mean spiritual elitism, but indicates ownership. God says, "You belong to Me!"

Paul continues in the first chapter of Ephesians, praying that the Christians may have the eyes of their understanding enlightened that they might know what is the hope of God's calling, and "what are the riches of the glory of *His inheritance in the saints..."* (Ephesians 1:18).

Then in the second chapter, the apostle declares that the Christians are God's workmanship: "By grace you have been saved through faith, and that not of yourselves; it is the gift of God, not of works, lest anyone should boast. *For we are His workmanship, created in Christ Jesus for good works, which God prepared beforehand that we should walk in them*" (Ephesians 2:8-9).

And then in Paul's prayer for the Ephesians in the third chapter, verses 17-19, we are given the astounding truth that saints are to be the postresurrection home of the living Christ: *"...that Christ may dwell in your hearts through faith; that you, being rooted and grounded in love, may be able to comprehend with all the saints what is the width and length and depth and height—to know the love of Christ which passes knowledge; that you may be filled with the fullness of God."*

From these descriptive phrases we discover what it means to be holy: we are the inheritance of God, His property, the workmanship of God, people He is shaping according to His plan and purpose, and the dwelling place of Christ, His home. Awesome indeed!

Say these truths to yourself until they sink in: "I am the Lord's property, I am His workmanship, and I am His home. I am not my own, I am His. The progression is stunning: the Lord's proprietorship, His possession, and His passion."

These are lofty thoughts, but what do they mean to us in the twenty-first century in the asphalt jungle? Nothing less than that all we are and have belongs to the Lord. This means our minds, emotions, wills, and bodies belong to Him. The reign of Christ in us includes the people, possessions, and plans of our lives. And we don't stop there.

Our list grows to include the memories that shape our present and the values that etch our future. In addition, we must be sure to include our work, where we spend most of our days. Most contemporary saints will work 160,000 hours in their lifetimes. If they take few vacations and work after hours, many of them will work about 200,000 hours. A housewife will work more than 290,000! Work can be either drudgery or a delight. The crucial question is, "Do we bring meaning to our work, or do we make our work the meaning of our lives?" If we accept that every facet of our lives is holy, then we can be assured that we are deployed in our place of employment to work for Christ on the job.

Choosing to be chosen as a saint means accepting Christ's Lordship over our total lives.

We not only belong, first and foremost, to the Lord, but because we belong to Him, we are His workmanship. The Greek word for workmanship is *poema*, which denotes "something that is made," and often refers to a thing of beauty and perfection. Our English word *poem* comes from this Greek word. A poem has flow, symmetry, order, and balance. We have been elected to be saints for nothing less. The Lord wants to shape the beautiful person He intends each of us to be and the good works He has planned for us to accomplish.

John Knox said, "God loveth us because we are His own handiwork."

Saints are people who are like clay on the eternal Potter's wheel. Watch the human artist-potter for the full impact of the biblical image (Jeremiah 18:2-6). He takes the clay and puts it on the wheel. His foot is pumping until the wheel is spinning. Then he places his hands on the clay. In the mind of the potter there is a vision of the vessel he is shaping for use and for beauty. As the wheel revolves the thought that is in the mind of the potter is being revealed in the clay. As clay is in the potter's hand, so are we in the Lord's hands. The Lord's hand is on the saints—molding, making, perfecting persons for His glory.

Once again, we are at the crux of sainthood. The true attitude is submission, yielding, surrender to the Potter's hand. The will to be willing is the secret of realizing the joy of sainthood. Tennyson was right:

> Our wills are ours, we know not how;
> Our wills are ours, to make them Thine.

And so was Adelaide Pollard when, after accepting God's will for her life instead of her own plans, she wrote,

> Have Thine own way, Lord! Have Thine own way!
> Thou art the potter, I am the clay.
> Mold me and make me after Thy will,
> While I am waiting, yielded and still.

We are programmed for progress. As Paul put it in his epistle to the Philippians, "Not that I have already attained, or am already perfected; but I press on that I may lay hold of that for which Christ Jesus has also laid hold of me" (Philippians 3:12). So the motto and mantra of the saint is, "What He wills, where He wills, how He wills, I will to obey."

And the Lord is not finished with any of us. Sainthood gives us an honorary membership in the PBPGINTWMY Club. The acrostic is, "Please Be Patient, God Is Not Through With Me Yet."

Next to accepting our sainthood, our most crucial decision is to open our hearts to be Christ's home.

Not just the vestibule, but every room. It is when Christ dwells in us that His passion becomes real to us. We know for ourselves the width, length, depth of His love for us. And we are able to reach out to others with empathy and healing.

C. Saints are faithful

Saints are not only chosen and belong to God, they are faithful. The adjective *faithful*, in Greek *pistos*, can mean either "having faith" or "being faithful." I think Paul intended both usages. A saint, really, is one who both receives and exercises faith. "The righteousness of God is revealed *from faith to faith [pisteos eis pistin]; as it is written, 'The just shall live by faith.'*" (Romans 1:17). Primary faith is the gift of the Holy Spirit that enables us to believe in Christ as Lord and Savior; particularized faith is given for moment-by-moment trust that the Lord will accomplish what He has promised He will do. As we discover what the Lord wants us to do we are given an infusion of specific faith that the Lord will be in time, on time, for our time of need to guide our steps and give us the strength and courage we need.

D. Saints are prepositionally positioned

The preposition *in* says it all. The saints to whom Paul wrote were *in* Christ and *in* Ephesus. One without the other would have been blasphemy. It was there in the "Vanity Fair" of the ancient world, filled with the syncretism of pagan religions with the cult of Diana, and the secularism of the silversmiths, that the saints were called to live out their sainthood.

Today, the local congregation of saints does not exist for itself, but for the world around it that desperately needs the Savior. The ministry of the laity, the priesthood of all believers, is inseparably linked to the sainthood of all believers. To be in Christ is to be in ministry.

All the saints in any congregation are in ministry by their confirmation as surely as pastors are by ordination. Over some 60 years as a clergyman, I never used the term *minister* for myself. On the front of worship bulletins beneath the name of the church, I would put the number of members as the ministers of the church and then the number of pastors. All Christ's people are ministers. We are all His servants, *douloi*, in our relationships, at work, and in society. There should never be a question whether anyone who believes in Christ is a minister. The question is, what *kind* of minister, and to what extent is a church member living out Christ's calling?

As I have tried to stress repeatedly throughout my ministry, we do not need to send the saints into the world; they are already there! The challenge is to help them realize that the Lord, not just their own preferences, has placed them in their neighborhoods, jobs, clubs, activities, and social structures and cities.

E. Saints are gifted people

We are not left alone to struggle in our sainthood. We are given the gifts of grace and peace. "Grace to you and peace from God our Father and the Lord Jesus Christ" (Ephesians 1:2). We hear the whisper in our souls, "You are loved unreservedly, your sins and failure have been washed away forever. Now live as a loved and forgiven person." There is no estrangement, no condemnation. Grace is the unqualified, unlimited, unfettered love of God.

I remember one evening when I was seated in the bleachers at the Edinburgh Castle. My blood was stirred by the pipes and drums, the marching bands, and the beautiful pageantry. As part of the evening's program, groups of people from all over the world were introduced. Then we were all invited to sing the hymn and popular song "Amazing Grace" in our own language. It was a delight to hear my favorite hymn sung in German, Japanese, and French—all blending in with the hearty voices of the Scots, who sang loudest of all.

A Highland Scots friend seated next to me tugged on my arm and exclaimed, "'Tis amazin', isn't it?" Thinking he meant the grace about which we were singing, I heartily agreed and began to talk enthusiastically about what grace meant to me and the peace I experienced as a result.

My friend interrupted my discourse. "Ach, that's not what I mean. Wat's amazin' is that everyone knows the song and is singing it together in thir own language."

I had to agree. That in itself was amazing, but for me the grace about which we were singing was and is the most amazing of all.

At the end of the tattoo that evening, a lone piper mounted the ramparts of the castle. All the lights were turned off except one spotlight that focused on him. He played the winsome, impelling melody of "Amazing Grace" once again. As the piper played with impeccable perfection, I reflected on what grace had meant to me all through the years.

I thought of the Scottish expression "Leal love," love that is loyal and indefatigable. It is also inexhaustible. We simply cannot diminish God's supply of grace. Receiving grace is like draining water from an ocean with a teaspoon. By grace God found us, by grace we received the gift of faith to respond, by grace we are given the confidence to cry out to Him when we are down, by grace He has intervened to help us, by grace we receive wisdom to know how to care for others, by grace we receive healing when we are ill, by grace we will die victoriously, and by grace we will live forever. As saints, we know grace heaped upon grace and grace. 'Tis amazin', isn't it!

When we receive grace as a gift of our sainthood, we hear a further whisper in our souls, "Peace to you!"

- Peace is the *essence* of the persistent, mind-staying power of God to bring us into, and keep us in, complete harmony between us and Him.

- Peace is the result of the *exoneration*, the forgiveness of past sins and failures. We are free! (Colossians 1:19-22).

- Peace is the *exhilaration* of the palpable presence of Christ. ("Peace I leave with you, My peace I give to you"—John 14:27 and Ephesians 2:14.)

- Peace is the *expectation* of the intervention of Christ. ("Lo, I am with you always"—Matthew 28:20.)

- Peace is the *experience* of reconciled relationships. ("Let the peace of Christ rule in your hearts"—Colossians 3:15.)

- Peace is an *expression* of the assurance of Christ's unimpeachable control around us and within us. ("Abide in Me, and I in you…"—John 15:4.)

- Peace is the *exuberance* of blessedness. ("Blessed are the peacemakers, for they shall be called sons of God"—Matthew 5:9.)

Thomas à Kempis prayed for peace with an understanding of the secret of receiving it:

> Lord Jesus, let Thy will be mine, and let my will always follow Thine, and agree perfectly therewith…Grant that I may rest in Thee above all things that can be desired, and that my heart may be at peace in Thee. Thou are the true peace of the heart, Thou art its only rest; out of Thee all things are irksome and restless. In this very peace which is in Thee, the one Supreme Good, I will sleep and take my rest…Amen.

Now, there's a great prayer from a saint in heaven for saints on earth today, not only for the end of each day, but for every moment of each day. And don't miss the reiteration of the salient secret of the surrender of the will: the saint's open secret to realizing the status and security and strength of our sainthood.

The sure sign of our sainthood is ongoing, ever-deepening, consistent realization and experience of grace and peace.

III. The Closing

I want to close with a rewording of one of the greatest hymns on saints in heaven. The problem with its historic wording is its tense. It extols the saints in heaven, but I like to reword some of it to capture what the sublime calling of sainthood means to you and me today.

> We are saints and do confess,
> And before the world profess,

Your name, O Jesus, we forever bless,
Alleluia, Alleluia!

You are our rock, our fortress, and our might,
You, Lord, our Captain in the well-fought fight,
In the darkness You are our one true light,
Alleluia, Alleluia!

O blest communion, fellowship divine,
Saints on earth and saints in glory shine;
All one in You, eternal life sublime,
Alleluia, Alleluia!

The future dawns, an even more glorious day;
Choosing to be chosen, we are willing to obey
Christ in us, our hope of glory, shows the way.
Alleluia, Alleluia!

Your Grace and Peace have helped us thrive
You never leave or forsake us, we survive,
Alleluia, Alleluia!

Chapter 10

Preaching to the Underwhelmed

Preaching at the special services of the Christian year presents us with a challenge. People often come with low expectation and ho-hum familiarity. Repetition of Scriptures, pet phrases, hymns and anthems, often leave them uninspired.

On a recent Good Friday evening I began a sermon with a straightforward introduction that identified this concern, and then went on to preach the following sermon. I include it in our discussion of passionate preaching as another example, because it was a different approach to a sermon on the cross than I have included in previous chapters. The sermon was entitled "Trembling at Calvary." Here it is for your reflection.

I. Introduction

There's a problem many of us face on Good Friday evening. It is not for me to tell you that you also have this problem, but in a moment of honest confession, you may realize that we share this common difficulty.

What I am suggesting is faithless familiarity. It is a proclivity: verbal and ritual repetition can give us a debilitated spiritual audio nerve. Great, life-changing, and affirming truths can become so familiar that the sound of them no longer reaches our mind, emotions, will. Leo Tolstoy was right: "Familiarity is the opiate of the imagination." It is also a dulling narcotic, debilitating the full realization of the grace offered to us at Calvary.

I remember overhearing a bored remark by a woman leaving a church sanctuary after a Good Friday service in which there had been stunning music and stimulating preaching. She exclaimed, "Well, I certainly was under-whelmed by that!" *Underwhelmed?* How could she be?

How very different from my mother who, when she thought about the crucifixion of Christ, would express with almost breathless intensity, "Oh, the wonder of it all!"

We are here tonight to hear, receive, and experience the sheer wonder of Calvary.

We hear a haunting, confrontive question that makes us a bit uneasy. And yet, each of us must answer it. The question comes from the old Afro-American spiritual that demands an answer: "Were you there when they crucified my Lord?"

We answer with the typical defensiveness we feel when-ever we are held accountable for hearing and acting on spir-itual truth: "Well, no, how could I have been there? Calvary was two thousand years ago!"

Our limited understanding of time and space is exposed. Christ, the Son of God, a preexistent Person of the Trin-ity, came incarnate into time and space to reconcile us to the Father. What happened on Calvary revealed the heart of God beyond the limits of time and space. Therefore, in the timeless love of God, the cross was then and it is now. If it was not then, it could not be now, but if it is not now, on this night, we have missed the profound, mind-boggling, heart-thumping, transforming, healing, affirming, liberating truth and experience of the cross.

Again the persistent question must be answered. Now the wording has changed slightly, but very significantly: *"Are you there as they crucify my Lord?"* And then comes the answer that must become our response: "Tonight, it causes me to tremble, tremble."

II. Body of Thought

A. Exposition

The apostle Paul encouraged the Christians at Philippi to "work out your own salvation with fear and trembling; for it is God who works in you both to will and to do for His good pleasure" (Philippians 2:12-30). We understand this in the context of Paul's Hebrew understanding of *fear* as awe, and *trembling* as a gripping outward expression of the impact of truth on our intellect, the inspiration of our emotions, and the instigation of our intentionality. Note carefully that Paul's admonition follows his stunning challenge:

> Let this mind be in you which was also in Christ Jesus, who, being in the form of God, did not consider it robbery to be equal with God, but made Himself of no reputation, taking the form of a bondservant, and coming in the likeness of men. And being found in appearance as a man, He humbled Himself and became obedient to the point of death, even the death of the cross. Therefore God has highly exalted Him and given Him the name which is above every name, that at the name of Jesus every knee should bow, of those in heaven, and of those on earth, and of those under the earth, and that every tongue should confess that Jesus Christ is Lord, to the glory of God the Father (Philippians 2:5-11).

Then the apostle goes on with the response required of those who really take seriously the example of Christ's self-emptying humility on the cross. Nothing less: Work out, live out, the salvation we have received with fear; that is, awe and trembling; that is, the full, unreserved realization of Christ's humility in our own lives.

That causes me to tremble, indeed! Especially when I grapple with the words, "Let this mind be in you which was also in Christ Jesus…" (verse 5). The Greek word Paul used for mind is *phroneistho* from *phroneo*, denoting what one has in mind, the thought; that is, the content of the process of thinking, to have in mind. The present passive imperative is used. It is for now, it is done to us, and we are to energetically pursue it. What is "it"?

Humility. Paul has presented Christ as the supreme example of humility and then urges the Christians at Philippi to emulate Christ's humility with awe and intentionality.

B. Application

Tonight we come to the cross and witness again Christ's humility and then respond to His challenge to take up our cross with humility. But don't miss the stunning fact that the word for humility in this verse is not the traditional word for humility, *tapeinophrosune*, but rather *ekenose*, meaning "to empty."

Christ emptied Himself. Of what did He empty Himself? Not His divine nature. Not His Godhood. That was impossible. He continued to be the Son of God. What He emptied Himself of was His divine power and authority to control the circumstances of His forthcoming crucifixion.

Christ took on the form of a servant and allowed His crucifixion as the once-never-to-be-repeated sacrifice for the sins of the world, yours and mine. In response to the guidance and authority of the Father, in the Garden of Gethsemane, Christ prayed, "Father, if it is Your will, take this cup away from Me; nevertheless not My will, but Yours, be done" (Luke 22:42). Christ allowed Himself to be a victim, to be victimized by the manipulation of the leaders of Israel and the cruelty of the Roman authorities and executioners.

At any moment Christ could have stopped the ignominious process, but out of obedience to the Father, and out of love for you and me, He went to the cross. Our Lord had stilled the waves of the sea, He had walked on water, He had changed water into wine, He had made the blind see and the lame walk, and most awesome, He had raised Lazarus from the dead. And yet, the divine Messiah humbled himself, took the form of a servant, accepted the irrevocable will of His Father, and went to the cross. I want to tell you, *that* makes me tremble!

All through the six excruciating hours of pain during the crucifixion, the words Christ spoke from the cross revealed the depth of His submission as the Lamb of God. He prayed that the Father would forgive His executioners, who drove the nails into His hand and feet. He identified with the abhorrent sense of human forsakenness and prayed the first verse of the twenty-second psalm: "God, why have You forsaken Me?"

And at the end of the hours of suffering, He cried out, "It is finished!" What was finished was the cosmic atonement, the in-time, for-all-time reconciliation of humankind to God. Then with His last breath Christ prayed a prayer from Psalm 31:5 that every Hebrew child had learned at his mother's knee: "Father, into Your hands I commit My spirit" (Luke 23:46). And that too causes us to tremble!

C. Response

And our response? To work out our salvation with fear and trembling, knowing that at the same time God is at work within us seeking to will and do for His good pleasure. For us, this means that we are never finished realizing what Christ has finished for us on Calvary. Every day is Calvary as we realize afresh the grace of the Lord Jesus flowing from the

Cross. His self-emptying motivates our self-emptying. And of what do I most need to be emptied?

Control! To a greater or lesser degree we are all control freaks, seeking to control what we were never meant to control, and refusing to take responsibility for what has been entrusted to us to manage under the Lord's moment-by-moment, controlling guidance and empowering. The opposite of trying to control people and circumstances is our own self-emptying, taking up our cross and dying to willful, imperious control. Then we can experience resurrection to a new life filled with the abiding Christ and His inner direction of what is maximum for us, and those we love, in all the ups and downs of life. And that wondrous offer to live life as it was meant to be lived also ought to cause us to tremble.

D. Challenge

There's hope for the control freaks tonight! We can give up running our segment of the universe and surrender our frustrated hearts to our Lord. It is abdication time for all of us who squeeze the joy out of life with the icy-cold fist of anxiety over not being in controlling charge of everything and everyone. We can enter what Louisa Fletcher Tarkington called "the Land of Beginning Again":

> I wish that there were some wonderful place
> Called the Land of Beginning Again,
> Where all our mistakes and all our heartaches
> And all our poor, selfish grief
> Could be dropped, like a shabby old coat, at the door,
> And never put on again.[24]

Calvary is that wonderful place of beginning again for us tonight. There's a tingling up my spine, a gripping flow of spectacular truth in my mind, and a surge of joyous emotion in my being when I think about the cross and close my eyes to see the cruel nails and crown of thorns and Christ crucified for me. But even could I have seen Him die, I could have seen only a part of that great love, which like a fire, is always burning in His heart.

III. Closing

And so tonight on what I like to call Grace Friday, we claim what is ours because of the cross:

We know our ultimate worth that Christ would die for us.

We know we are loved absolutely and utterly.

We know that we have been forgiven for all that we have said and done to break the Savior's heart and hurt the people of our lives.

We have been set free of guilt and remorse.

We have been chosen, cherished, and called to be Christ's disciples.

We know He will be with us in all the ups and downs of life.

We have been commissioned to take up our own cross, to empty ourselves of our control of the people, circumstances, possessions, and plans of our lives and commit them to Christ to work out for His glory and our growth.

We have been elected to be transformed into the image of Christ and filled with His abiding presence.

We know the joy of being part of the church, the Body of Christ, and know the delight of oneness with our fellow disciples.

We have been given the privilege of communicating His love and forgiveness to the people of our lives.

We are called to serve the lost and lonely, hungry and homeless, debilitated and distressed people of the world and work tirelessly for justice and righteousness in the world.

We are alive forever; death will be only a transition in our eternal life. Heaven for us has begun!

All this and so much more is ours because of the cross.

And tonight, you and I are there. And that causes us to tremble!

Chapter 11

Finishing Well

The four forbidden words for the passionate preacher are, "And now, in conclusion." Preaching should be dialogical, not monological. It is meant to be part of a continuing conversation between a pastor and the congregation. Finishing a sermon well communicates a "let's talk" receptivity in the passionate preacher.

In a good conversation between two people or among a group of people, we wouldn't end our input or response by saying, "And now, in conclusion." Who would want to be part of a conversation that is one-sided and abruptly ended by a long-winded participant who presumed that when he or she was finished, an appropriate ending would be to declare a conclusion!

And yet, I am convinced that's what happens when we think of a sermon as an independent, stand-alone presentation rather than one more step in a continuing conversation between the preacher and people. If our preaching is truly a response to listening to the deepest needs and most urgent questions of our people, then ending the sermon must be done in a way that communicates that it is one part of an ongoing exchange between people—congregants who think of their input as a trusting request for insight and wisdom, and us who think of our response in the sermon as an answer of love and encouragement, steeped in hours of study and prayer.

Having said all that about the four forbidden words, *how do we close a sermon well?*

You will not be surprised that I strongly suggest that the last paragraphs of the sermon be carefully written and polished and then committed to memory. The reason for this is that we can ramble on past the point of effectiveness trying to finish on time. A carefully prepared ending allows for the Lord to add Scripture references, illustrations, and ideas to the final pages of our message we had not thought of in our hours in the study. We are relaxed enough to receive these sublime moments when we are confident that what we have prepared to finish with will be augmented by the Lord. We are free to give an eye-to-eye, stunning, and challenging completion of the message.

Parenthetically, I honestly want to affirm that those added inspirations from the Lord are the parts of the sermon about which people most often comment. A woman leaving the sanctuary one Sunday morning exclaimed, "You bugged our house! There's no other way you could have known what we've been through this past week! What you said was the answer my husband and I really needed. It was as if the Lord spoke directly to us."

Well, in fact, He had! I told her what had happened, that I had been interrupted by the Lord with the liberating insight I had not prepared before that moment!

But I also have to admit to myself that those supernatural moments most often happen when I have done my homework on the introduction, body of thought, and final paragraphs and enter into the pulpit with the prayer, "Lord, I trust that You have guided what I am about to preach. Add to it or subtract from it. You know infinitely more about my people. Speak through me, Lord!"

Unashamedly, I can say He has answered that prayer all through 60 years of preaching. So often, I sense His accelerating, instigating courage as I reach the final paragraphs of the sermon.

The Thrust and Purpose of the Ending

The purpose of the end of the sermon is to help people act on what we have preached. When I was pastor of the First Presbyterian Church of Hollywood, a house across the intersection from the main exit from the sanctuary was occupied by a group that announced its name on a large sign: "The Do It Now Society." As I shook hands with people leaving the sanctuary, I'd often point to the sign as I responded to their comments about wanting to live out what I'd preached about in the sermon. "Do it now! Today, tomorrow, this week!" I'd say. "Okay, okay!" some would exclaim. Others would respond more circumspectly, "I'll do my best, Pastor; see you next Sunday!"

Another important aspect of finishing the sermon well is to end with spiritual intensity and crescendo. If a message is worth preaching, it is worthy of a stirring final paragraph that leads people to honest confession, deep conviction, and renewed commitment.

I think of the young preacher who asked his bishop to sit in his congregation and critique his sermon. After the service, he asked the bishop, "Well, how'd I do?" "Do!" the bishop responded with consternation. "That's just the problem. Your sermon didn't *do* anything! It was humorous in places, informative in others, but I didn't feel compelled to do or attempt anything in response."

The ending of a sermon should leave people face-to-face with Christ. Remember, He is the Glorifier of the Father in the church, and He is the instigator of action, growth, and application. It is helpful for us to verbally step out of the way in the culminating paragraphs and remind people that we have sought to preach the Word of the Lord and He is the one with Whom we and they must deal. He wants to know: what are we going to do about what He has said to us?

Also, in a sermon in which we have attempted to explain a verse or passage where the Lord offers an aspect of His grace, it is very important to ask people if they have accepted the gift. Our calling is to help them imagine what life would be like if they did.

Varied Methods for Varied People

Today we preach to congregations made up of people who made a commitment to Christ years ago, others who need to commit concerns and challenges they are facing, and still others who may believe in Christ, but have never committed their lives to him. The final moments of a sermon must take seriously these varied groups of people. I have found it helpful honestly to acknowledge the diversification and ask each group separately for a response of a first-time commitment, a renewed commitment, or a deeper commitment to what the thrust of the message from the Scripture has demanded.

> The closing moments should be moving, motivating, and leave a congregation longing for more, even if they have to wait for the forthcoming sermon the following Sunday.

Ending the sermon with a strongly worded quote is a very helpful way to finish with strength. When I finish a sermon with the theme of a commitment to Christ we've just discussed or a commitment to act on convictions about discipleship renewed throughout the body of thought of the sermon, I like to close with a quote that is based on some of the words of Goethe:

> The moment one definitely commits oneself, then Providence moves too. All sorts of things occur to help one that would never otherwise have occurred. A whole stream of events issues from the decision, raising in one's favor all manner of unforeseen incidences and meetings and material assistance, which no one could have dreamed would come his way. "Whatever you can do, or dream you can do, begin it. Boldness has genius, power, and magic in it." Begin it now![25]

Further, living the abundant life is an exciting adventure. There's always another step in discovering and doing the Lord's will. Ending a sermon on this theme should encourage people to press on. There are times when I have been led to ask, "If you loved Christ with all your heart, what would you do about what He has called us to do this morning? What difference would it make in your marriage, your family, at work, and in the challenges we all face living for Him in this materialistic, secularized, society that worships the perpendicular pronoun? What's the next step for you? Christ has made it clear for each of us. I'm ready. How about you?"

My great friend, the late Dr. Bruce Larson (whom I mentioned earlier), for years the pastor of the University Presbyterian Church in Seattle, Washington, had an incisive way of finishing sermons in churches or talks at conferences: "If you knew you could not fail, what would you do to live what I've tried to communicate about your faith at work in your relationship with God, yourself, others, and the world?"

Bruce was a Copernican thinker and preacher and a leader of relational Christianity. He was able to talk about what it meant to follow Christ in today's world. He led thousands of people to the Savior by asking them to live on what he called "the edge of adventure" in a life-affirming, personal relationship with Him.

The methods of finishing the sermon need to be varied, just as the introductions or the number of points in the body of thought need to be diversified to avoid predictability and the boredom of sameness. The closing moments should be moving, motivating, and leave a congregation longing for more, even if they have to wait for the forthcoming sermon the following Sunday.

The "take away method" for ending a message is effective. This can be done in two ways: by simply asking people what they will take away from what we have tried to communicate in the sermon; the other is to list the main points of the message and share with the people that these can be their take-away inspiration from the message.

Presently, I am a part of a very dynamic group of men who meet twice each month as a covenant group to study the Bible, share their needs and hopes, and pray for one another. At the ending of each meeting they have what they call "take-away time." Going around the group each one is asked to share what he will take with him from the time together. This has helped them to articulate what the Lord has inspired in their minds and hearts during the meeting, and also to enable the group to help them be accountable in putting what they had discovered into action in their homes and offices. After being apart between meetings, they look each other in the eye and ask for a report on how they have, or have not, followed through.

Another effective ending of a sermon is a life story of a person who has faithfully lived what we have preached in the body of thought of the message.

I enjoy ending with a poem, especially when I have learned about the circumstances in which the poem was written that are directly applicable to the thrust of the message. One of my favorite poets is Annie Johnson Flint. She endured crippling arthritis that finally caused her to be bedridden. During this time she wrote some of her most powerful poems. Her family would prop her up with as many as 12 pillows and press into her gnarled right hand a pen so she could write.

One of these poems was about the infinite resources of God in Christ given to us in our times of deepest needs. Often when I preach on James 4:6, "He giveth more grace" (KJV), I end by describing the circumstances under which the poem was written and then repeating it from memory. A poem like this deserves to be memorized so it can be given with great feeling, again with eye-to-eye contact motivated by a heart filled with the grace we've made every effort to explain:

> He giveth more grace when the burdens grow greater,
> He sendeth more strength when the labors increase;
> To added affliction He addeth His mercy,

To multiplied trials, His multiplied peace.
When we have exhausted our store of endurance,
When our strength has failed ere the day is half done,
When we reach the end of our hoarded resources,
Our Father's full giving is only begun.

His love has no limit, His grace has no measure,
His power no boundary known unto men;
For out of His infinite riches in Jesus
He giveth and giveth and giveth again![26]

A contemporary poet by the name of Sue McCollum organized a movement for cancer research called "My Blue Dots" after she suffered from cancer and bore the reminders with her own blue dots marking where she had had radiation treatment.

One day Sue and her husband, Bob, attended a worship service in Palm Springs during which I preached on "The Red Ember in the White Ash." The sermon was about the way the Lord puts a bellows on the white ash in the hearth of our hearts and billows the flickering red ember into a flame of passion again. Now, whenever I preach about the billows of the Lord, I have Sue's permission to finish with this moving poem about what happened to her to set her faith burning brightly again. I quoted it at the closing of the first chapter of my book *The Red Ember in the White Ash*:

Within my heart is a red ember
where once a fire used to be.
A small red ember amidst the white ash
is all that's inside of me.

My heart used to be a mighty blaze,
I had great passion for the Lord,
I thought I could conquer mountains,
but now I sit here bored.

The blaze became a little flame,
and then a small red ember,
Lost I was in the white ash,
my God I could hardly remember.

But God did not let me go,
but on that ember He blew,
He set my heart aflame again
and created me anew.[27]

Calling for a Response: An Invitation for Healing

In chapter 4 I talked about providing a time for prayers for healing during the singing of the hymn of dedication after the sermon. The invitation for people to come forward to kneel and receive prayer for healing of spiritual, emotional, relational, problematical, and physical needs can be blended with the final paragraphs of the sermon and the call for specific response to the thrust of the exposition.

When I speak of healing, I do not use the word for physical healing alone. In the New Testament, the word healing is used to communicate the many aspects of wholeness. The basic Greek word is *sozo,* the root from which both *save* and *salvation* come. It is also translated as "to make whole." Christ came to save us from our sins, complete our salvation on Calvary, and live with and in us to make us whole people in every facet of life. He heals us of spiritual estrangement and reconciles us to the Father for eternity. Remember, we are the chosen, called, and cherished saints of God.

And yet, we acquire mental, emotional, volitional, and physical diseases that cripple us in living the abundant life fully. Christ, the Glorifier in the church, would not want any person to leave a worship service without an opportunity to ask for the healing of their souls or the soul-sized physical or spiritual issues he or she is facing. He wants to do for all of us, preacher and people, what He did for the man by the Pool of Bethesda: "I made a man completely well…" (John 7:23). The King James Version has it, "I have made a man every whit whole…"

Having a time for the healing of the manifold needs of people requires the training of the elders and deacons and others in leadership who have asked for and received the gift of praying for people. They need to learn how to look a person in the eye with empathy and ask, "For what may I pray?" and then to pray a prayer that puts the person in direct relationship with Christ.

There are so few places today where people can admit their longing to meet Christ or commit their needs to Him and receive His healing. Why not in our churches?

Whatever method of finishing the sermon for any one Sunday we may utilize, it needs to be done with the tone and tenor of what I like to call "Let's talk about it" openness. This makes a sermon a part of the ongoing conversation between us and our people and affirms that we are ready to hear their responses and further questions and think and pray about them in the preparation of subsequent sermons.

We can finish well and press on with enthusiasm and excitement!

Chapter 12

Playing Catch in the Pulpit:
Dialogical Preaching

Writing and then delivering a sermon for me is like playing catch. As I am writing, I think of throwing a ball. It must be straight for the catcher's mitt, the minds and hearts of the people assembled in the sanctuary. Then I think of waiting for the return of the ball, the response on people's faces, the nod of their heads, the growing intensity of their body language as their hearts say "S-t-r-i-k-e!" At the same time I hope to avoid a ho-hum, thumbs-down "B-a-l-l."

To stretch the image further, I never want to see in people's faces a "Ball four—walk!" Most of all, I want my Coach (the Lord) to keep me in the game: pitching the truth and catching the return throw of people's response indicating intellectual understanding and spiritual acceptance.

This practice of playing imaginary catch while writing the body of thought of the sermon prepares me to continue the same mental give and take and expression while preaching the sermon. Preaching dialogically enables us to be able to read the level of the response of our people. When we sense that they are with us and are understanding what the Lord has put on our minds and hearts to communicate from the biblical text, we can press on at their pace that sometimes is way ahead of us.

One Key Factor in the Presentation

Our search for the factors that contribute to preaching with passion brings us to an analysis of the presentation of the sermons we labor so diligently to write, pray over, and review repeatedly until they are nearly memorized. As we have stressed throughout this book, preaching is getting the message as a living reality into other minds. Our high calling is to get the Word of the Lord out of our hearts and into the hearts of people. That requires a passionate preacher, one who is warm, joyous, hopeful, enthusiastic, vulnerable, and free to give away himself or herself contagiously in communicating grace. That requires eye contact. Having our faces buried in our manuscript makes that impossible. I learned that the hard way. Allow me to share how that happened.

When I was just starting my ministry in Winnetka, Illinois, the newly organized Winnetka Presbyterian Church had no church building and met in a school auditorium. My study was in a third-floor attic of my house on Vernon Street, half a mile from the school.

In those early days, I wrote out a complete manuscript of my sermon and read it word for word with my head buried in it while preaching. Then one Sunday morning catastrophe struck…or so I thought!

I had gotten up early to put the final touches on the manuscript of the sermon. I became so engrossed in my work that I lost track of time. Suddenly I was startled to realize it was almost time for the church service to begin. So I gathered up my precious pages of manuscript, stuck them in my Bible, and threw my preaching robe over my arm. I ran down the steps from the attic, then on to the main stairs, and out of the front door toward my car parked in the driveway. Greatly agitated by my lateness, I rushed to the car, opened the back door, placed my Bible and my manuscript on the roof, hung up my preaching robe inside, slammed the door, and got into the driver's seat.

Totally forgetting where I had placed my Bible and manuscript, I started the car, hurriedly backed out into the street, and zoomed off to the school. While I drove at a speed that surely must have exceeded the limit, first the pages of my manuscript and then the pages of my Bible were scattered all along the street and the front lawns of the neighborhood. I had answered the call to come to the community to share the Word of God, but not in this way!

When I reached school, I got out of my car, opened the back door, and realized I had my preaching robe, but no Bible—and no manuscript I was totally dependent on to read from the pulpit that morning!

Remembering how late I was, I raced to a room at the side of the platform of the auditorium where I was to meet with the elders to pray. Breathlessly, I rushed into the room realizing that I had no Bible from which to read my text, no manuscript to read as my sermon, and no printed order of worship to guide me through the service.

There was nothing I could do but apologize for being late, and with an embarrassed, red face, I asked if I could borrow one of the elders' Bibles. With a warm smile and twinkle in his eye, the elder asked, "Pastor, don't you own a Bible?" We all laughed and the pressure oozed out of me. With a great need for divine help to lead the worship and preach, I got on my knees. The elders laid hands on my head and shoulders and prayed for me and what was ahead in the next hour.

Fortified by the time of prayer, I went out on the stage of the auditorium and up to the speaking stand that served as the makeshift pulpit. I looked into the eager, expectant faces of my congregation gathered in the seats in the front of the auditorium. Then I gave a call to worship and all the rest of the opening portions of the service fell into place, including the extemporaneous prayers that flowed with freedom and the hymns I remembered I had selected for that morning. After swallowing hard, I read the Scripture from my borrowed Bible.

But now it was time to preach. I prayed and took a deep breath. Then I spoke the topic sentence on which I had worked so long the previous week. I was delighted that repeated polishing and reading out loud of the paragraphs of the introduction enabled me to speak them without hesitation. The points of the body of thought also had had careful preparation and I moved from one to the other with ease that both surprised and excited me. When I reached the conclusion, again I realized that all the hard work of the week before paid off. I was able to remember most of it and finish the sermon with Christ-given strength.

The thing that was so satisfying about this fledgling attempt to preach without a manuscript was that I saw the faces of my people during a sermon for the first time! I had tasted the delight of dialogical preaching! This delight and the affirmation of my people made me determined to never go back to reading a sermon manuscript.

That was some 55 years ago. Since then the most I have ever brought into the pulpit is one page of reminders of the main points of the body of thought and any longer quotations I wanted to give exactly as they had been written or spoken. Usually, what's on the page has become so much a part of me that I seldom depend on reading it.

> People will feel they are in a personal conversation with us. There will be directness, urgency, and reality that will produce a living encounter of mind with mind, heart with heart.

Our written manuscript should be so much a part of us that we can go into the pulpit with a single page of notes, or none at all. By reading our manuscript over out loud at least ten times, our auditory nerves will utilize the repetition until we get a sure grip on our carefully written words and our optic nerves have taken a picture of each paragraph and page to store in our cerebral cortex.

All this depends on having a manuscript with logical structure, well-defined divisions and subdivisions, short paragraphs with a single, clear-cut thought in each, balance and progress in the development, and vivid illustrations providing windows open to the truth.

If our sermon stands out clearly in all its parts before our own mind, the tyranny of the manuscript is broken. This freedom gives preaching a dialogical dynamic. People will feel they are in a personal conversation with us. There will be directness, urgency, and reality that will produce a living encounter of mind with mind, heart with heart. There will be an arresting verve, and an impelling intensity.

To be sure, the first times you go into the pulpit to preach without a manuscript, it will feel like leaping out of an aircraft without a parachute. But don't forget: "Underneath are the everlasting arms!"

The Assurance of Christ's Power

With the assurance that Christ the Glorifier in the church is present during the preaching pouring out His power, then there is no need for anxiety, pretentiousness, or posturing. We do not need a "stained-glass" voice or any theatrical affectations. A famous actor remarked, "Tell your preaching friends to leave the acting to us. Tell us about God and how we can know Him!"

Gestures can be used sparingly and never as a substitute for strength of profound exposition of the text. Our eye contact will be intense, our manner winsome, and our demeanor humble. We can be totally free of self-consciousness. Our motto can be "Without God we can't; without us He won't!"

I remember talking to a young clergyman about his lack of freedom in the pulpit. He said he felt confined and restrained. I asked that the two of us go into the sanctuary of his church, and I requested him to stand in the beautiful Gothic pulpit. From my place in a pew, all I could see were his upper chest and head. So I gathered up four hymnals and placed them on the floor of the pulpit and asked him to stand on them and give what he could remember of the sermon he had preached the Sunday before. After he finished, he said, "I'm free!" You can be sure that a carpenter raised the floor of the pulpit before the next Sunday.

The secret is to worship with the congregation. The gift of humility is given only as we ourselves express praise, truly confess, accept absolution, surrender burdens, receive hope, and experience a fresh anointing of the Holy Spirit in the prayer before the preaching of the sermon.

After that we are ready to offer the sermon as an act of worship. Our words will come forth throbbing with a fervor and reality totally unlike an overdramatic, pretentious, and self-conscious oratory. We do not have to impress others with our grasp of the truth or our commitment to the social gospel; we don't change people by our elocution or heal sick souls with our nifty nostrums. Christ is the only one who can meet people's needs! He is ready to speak through us if we ask Him.

James Denney said, "No man can give at once the impression that he himself is clever and that Jesus Christ is mighty to save." I really believe that. I first read that quote in a pastor's study in Scotland before I was ushered out to preach. The quote is on my mind every time I enter a pulpit.

I remember a time a number of years ago when I was seated on the platform waiting to preach in a Sunday morning service at the Ocean Grove Tabernacle in Ocean Grove, New Jersey, on the Atlantic coast. Suddenly, I heard a rumbling that sounded like a hurricane coming in off the ocean.

"What's happening?" I asked a man seated next to me. "Oh, don't worry," he responded, "The organist has just pulled out all the stops!" He pointed to the ceiling where the tongue-and-groove boards of the ceiling were rattling together under the force of a stirring rendition of "A Mighty Fortress Is Our God."

When I got up to preach, I heard an "Inner Voice" articulate a very crucial question: "What do you think it would be like if you pulled out all the stops during your sermon this morning?" My prayerful response was, "I'm ready, Lord!" What followed was 25 very exciting minutes of preaching. I think of that morning so often just before I preach now.

Great things can happen when we pull out all the stops. We are challenged to bring all we have and are—our study of the biblical text, theological insight, research, plus our training, talents, toil, and sweat of brain and heart—and consecrate it all to Christ the Glorifier, and then stand back and watch Him work.

Preaching with Passion in Today's World

Now before I finish writing this preacher-to-preacher book, there are some disturbing questions that linger and long to be answered by you and me, once and for all.

Can Christ use men and women today to preach with passion? If we give priority to preparation and prayer, if we really believe that the Word of God preached by the power of the Holy Spirit is indeed the Word of God, if we have no other purpose than to bring men and women into a vital encounter with the living Christ, if we throw caution to the wind and preach each sermon as if never to preach again, and if we leave all the results up to the Lord—can we preach with power and see lives changed, the church renewed, and society impacted by the ministry of a transformed, Christ-empowered laity? Yes, we can! But not without a renewed commitment to preaching as the pastor's highest calling. P.T. Forsyth was right: "With preaching Christianity stands or falls."

We affirm that with preaching the growth and effectiveness of a congregation stands or falls. And most salient of all, with preaching the ministry of a parish pastor succeeds or fails.

Preaching with passion—if not now, when? If not from the pulpits of our time, where? If not by you and me, then by whom?

Thomas Carlyle's description of the writing of his book on the French Revolution focuses our vision for preaching. One day when he finished the manuscript, he placed it on the floor near the fireplace. While he was on a walk, his maid came to clean. She thought the pile of pages of the manuscript was rubbish and threw it all in the fireplace. When Carlyle returned from his walk, he realized that he had to begin all over. It was worth it. The result was a magnificent literary accomplishment. "This I can tell the world," declared Carlyle, "that not for a hundred years have you had a book which has come so direct and flaming from the heart of a living man!"

May our people say nothing less of our preaching: "We have heard the gospel direct and flaming from the heart of a preacher who preaches with power and passion."

At the height of his leadership of the Scottish Reformation, John Knox exclaimed the prayer, "Give me Scotland or I die!"

My prayer is, "Give us passionate preachers so the church may not just survive, but thrive!"

John Wesley said, "Give me one hundred preachers who fear nothing but sin and desire nothing but God and such alone will shake the gates of hell and set up the kingdom of God on earth."

Wesley said of his own preaching, "I came into the town and gave them Christ!" He was in good company with the apostle Paul, who wrote the Christians at Rome, "I am persuaded that neither death nor life, nor angels nor principalities nor powers, nor things present nor things to come, nor height nor depth, nor any other created thing, shall be able to separate us from the love of God which is in Christ Jesus our Lord" (Romans 8:37-39).

With a smile on my face and a song of joy in my heart, I do not plan to write a closing paragraph with the words "And now, in conclusion"!

You and I are bound inseparably to one another by Christ and His passionate calling of us to preach. I am still learning every day in my study and every time I enter a pulpit what it means to preach with passion. I know you are too. No other calling is more challenging and demanding, and yet, more thrilling.

So give it all you've got and Christ will give you more than you ever imagined. And with the Glorifier with you there as you preach, you can give your people...heaven!

Notes

1. Thomas F. Torrance, *The Mediation of Christ* (Edinburgh: T and T Clark, 1992), pp. 117, 118-119.

2. From the hymn "It Is a Thing Most Wonderful," words by William W. How (1872). First verse added by anonymous.

3. R.C.H. Lenski, *Interpretation of I and II Corinthians* (Minneapolis, MN: Augsburg Publishing House, 1937,1963), 948-949.

4. Teresa Watanabe, "Protestants no longer a majority of Americans, study finds," *Los Angeles Times*, October 9, 2012, at http://articles.latimes.com/2012/oct/09/local/la-me-protestants-20121010; based on "Nones on the Rise," Pew Research Religion & Public Life Project, October 9, 2012, at www.pewforum.org/2012/10/09/nones-on-the-rise.

5. Some portions of this chapter were previously published in Lloyd J. Ogilvie, *Enjoying God* (Waco, TX: Word Publishing, 1989).

6. John Henry Jowett, *My Daily Meditation* (New York: Fleming H. Revell Company, 1914), April 13, p. 104.

7. John Henry Jowett, *The Preacher: His Life and Work* (New York: G.H. Doran, 1912), p. 133.

8. Leslie D. Weatherhead, *That Immortal Sea: And 16 Other Messages Upholding Christ as the Answer to Man's Deepest Needs* (New York: Abingdon Press, 1953), p. 191.

9. Gerald Kennedy, *His Word Through Preaching* (New York: Harper and Bros., 1947), p. 58.

10. Robert J. McCracken, *The Making of the Sermon* (New York: Harper & Bros., 1956) p. 90.

11. John Pudney, *John Wesley and His World* (New York: Charles Scribner's Sons, 1978), p. 101.

12. D. Macwilliam, *The Life of George Matheson* (London: Hodder and Stoughton, 1907), p. 181.

13. Quoted in John Crew Taylor, *The Blind Seer, George Matheson* (London: Vision Prose, 1960), p. 170. Portions of this quote are traced to a sermon by James Black that is included in his book *Days of My Autumn* (London: Hodder and Stoughton, 1950), p. 223.

14. Lloyd J. Ogilvie, *Climbing the Rainbow* (Waco, TX: Word Publishing, 1993), pp. 15-18.

15. Arthur John Gossip, *From The Edge of the Crowd* (Edinburgh: T and T Clark, 1924), p. 123.

16. From unpublished papers about Martyn Lloyd-Jones provided by James I. Packer, quoted

in *20 Centuries of Great Preaching: An Encyclopedia of Preaching*, vol. 11 (Waco, TX: Word Books, 1971), pp. 269-270.

17. Alexander Gammie, *Preachers I Have Heard* (London: Pickering & Inglis, n.d.), p. 197.

18. This chapter was drawn from "Introducing the Sermon," a chapter I contributed to the book *Handbook of Contemporary Preaching*, ed. Michael Duduit (Nashville, NT: Broadman Press, 1992). © Copyright 1992 Broadman Press. All rights reserved. Reprinted and used by permission of Lifeway Publishers, Nashville, TN.

19. Robert Browning, *Men and Women*, reprint ed. (Ann Arbor, MI: Scholarly Publishing Office, University of Michigan Library, 2005).

20. George Bernard Shaw, *Preface to Androcles and the Lion: On the Prospects of Christianity*, first published 1912 (Rockville, MD: IndyPublish, 2009).

21. C.S. Lewis, *Mere Christianity* (New York: HarperCollins, 1952, 1980).

22. Henry Drummond, *The Greatest Thing in the World and 21 Other Addresses by Henry Drummond* (London: Collins, 1930; ed. G.F. Maine and J.Y. Simpson, 1953).

23. F.B. Meyer, *Expository Preaching Plans and Methods* (New York: George H. Doran Co., 1912), p. 29.

24. From Louisa Fletcher Tarkington, "The Land of Beginning Again," *The Smart Set* magazine, August 1911, p. 38.

25. Adapted from W.H. Murray, *The Scottish Himalaya Expedition* (1951). Murray quotes a passage from Goethe's *Faust* (214-230), as freely translated and paraphrased by John Anster, 1835. The research on the origin of this quotation is summarized at www.goethesociety.org/pages/quotescom.html.

26. Annie Johnson Flint (1866–1932), Annie Johnson Flint, *Poems*, vol. 1 Grand Rapids, MI: Zondervan Publishing House, 1944), p. 54.

27. © Copyright 2004 Sue McCollum. Used by permission.

Other Inspiring Resources from Lloyd John Ogilvie

God's Best for My Life
A Classic Daily Devotional

As you meet with God day-by-day, His supernatural life will become real to you and in you. He will grant you His best for your life...

- friendship with Him that overcomes loneliness
- courage and endurance for life's challenges and adventures
- guidance when you're uncertain
- real love and affection for people—even those you have a tough time with
- inner peace that comes from the assurance He's always there

These 365 profoundly personal devotions invite you to discover, explore, and enjoy the incalculable blessing and love that wait for you when you spend time with the Father.

Experiencing the Power of the Holy Spirit
You Can Live God's Best Each Day

God has chosen you to be in close friendship with Him. He wants you to live within the intimate circle of the Father, the Son—*and* the Holy Spirit. In a very personal and practical way, Lloyd John Ogilvie reveals the secrets of living day by day in the power of the Spirit—the One who

- never sleeps, is always available, and never gives up on you
- helps you know the Father's will for you and guides your decisions
- provides a steady flow of strength for living with joy in the stress of life

As you accept the Holy Spirit's daily, hourly, moment-by-moment guidance, you will experience Him as your Counselor, Advocate, and Companion.

Praying Through the Tough Times

Do you feel exhausted or disturbed by the difficulties of life and relationships? Are you finding it difficult to pray?

From his own experience, longtime pastor Lloyd John Ogilvie offers words of hope for those times when your own words fail. Sixty encouraging, heart-opening prayers will help you reconnect with the God who cares about you and wants to comfort you. As you come to Him, He will guide you from panic to His perspective…and then to peace.

Quiet Moments with God

These daily, heartfelt prayers will help you nurture a special intimacy with God. You will experience God's blessed assurance as you are comforted by His boundless love and His promises to provide guidance and give strength.

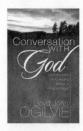

Conversation with God
Experience the Life-Changing Impact of Personal Prayer

Bestselling author Lloyd John Ogilvie shows you a fresh approach to prayer—one that is as much listening as speaking. He clearly and simply explains prayer's many dimensions and provides a 30-day guide so you can begin experiencing give-and-take conversation with God as part of your everyday life.

When You Need a Miracle
Experiencing the Power of the God of the Impossible

Are your greatest needs—with family, work, relationships—going unmet? Are you limiting your life to only what is possible in your own strength and talents? From his longtime pastoral experience, Dr. Ogilvie points the way to the God who can meet your every need because He is Lord of the *im*possible—the One who can bring about miracles of healing, reconciliation, and growth!